Dead
Biker

ALSO BY JERRY LANGTON

Biker: Inside the Notorious World of an Outlaw Motorcycle Gang

Fallen Angel: The Unlikely Rise of Walter Stadnick and the Canadian Hells Angels

Fighter: The Unauthorized Biography of Georges St-Pierre, UFC Champion

Gangland: The Rise of the Mexican Drug Cartels from El Paso to Vancouver

Outlaw Biker: The Russian Connection

Rage: The True Story of a Sibling Murder

Showdown: How the Outlaws, Hells Angels and Cops Fought for Control of the Streets

Dead Biker

INSIDE THE VIOLENT WORLD OF THE MEXICAN DRUG CARTELS

by

JERRY LANGTON

WILEY

John Wiley & Sons Canada, Ltd.

Library and Archives Canada Cataloguing in Publication Data

Langton, Jerry, 1965-
    Dead biker : inside the violent world of the Mexican drug cartels / Jerry Langton.

Issued also in electronic formats.
ISBN 978-1-118-14642-2

    1. Aiken, Ned.   2. Gang members—United States—Biography.
3. Motorcycle gangs—United States.   4. Drug dealers—Mexican-American Border Region—Biography.   5. Drug traffic—Mexican-American Border Region I. Title.

HV6439.U5L35 2012   364.106'6092   C2011-908045-1

ePDF: 978-1-118-14686-6; Mobi: 978-1-118-14687-3;
ePub: 978-1-118-14688-0

Production Credits
Cover design: Adrian So
Typesetting: Thomson Digital
Cover image: Thinkstock/iStockphoto
Printer: Trigraphik LBF

Editorial Credits
Executive editor: Don Loney
Managing editor: Alison Maclean
Production editor: Jeremy Hanson-Finger

John Wiley & Sons Canada, Ltd.
6045 Freemont Blvd.
Mississauga, Ontario
L5R 4J3

Printed in Canada

1 2 3 4 5 LBF TRI 16 15 14 13 12

Contents

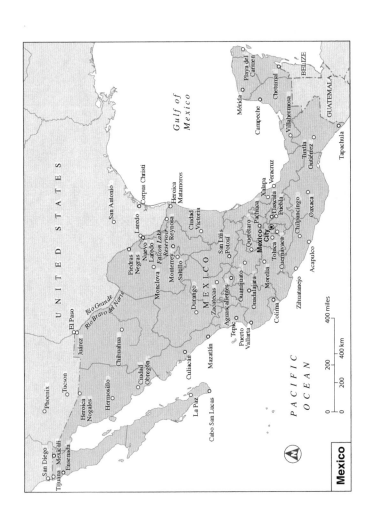

Mexico

Acknowledgments

After three books, several years, a number of countries, dozens of adventures, and countless close scrapes, Ned "Crash" Aiken has finally finished his long journey. Of course, he could not have made it had he not been assisted by an incredible team.

The obvious person to thank is Don Loney, everyone's favorite editor and bluesman. Without Don, I couldn't put two words together with any level of confidence. After him, the guy to thank would be Brian Will, who keeps everything running.

It would be inconceivable not to thank Robert Harris, who somehow took a proposal to record a biker cop's memoirs and made it into a fictional account of what it's like to be a biker. And, of course, I have to thank my agent and best pal, BG Dilworth, who (in his distinctive Southern drawl) told me: "Y'all ought to make this a series—y'know, write a sequel or two."

Others who deserve thanks after working on the book include slick marketers Erin Kelly and the formidable Robin Dutta-Roy, managing editor Alison Maclean (who said the nicest thing I have ever heard about my writing), production editor Jeremy Hanson-Finger, and cover designer Adrian So for his usual awesome job.

Of course, Ned's adventures would not have been possible if it were not for the brave efforts of the journalists, police officers, lawyers, and others I have spoken with. They allowed me to get a much better understanding of how organized crime works in Mexico and Eastern Europe and how it affects us in North America.

I also must thank Leta Potter because it would be dangerous not to.

Finally, I have to thank my family—Tonia, Damian and Hewitt—for all their patience and suggestions.

Chapter One

Ned's heart sank when he saw the cops at the corner. The police had set up a random checkpoint just a few feet from where he was stuck in traffic, and he hadn't seen it until it was too late. As they had all over Mexico, including his dusty and slow-moving new hometown of Nogales, just south of the Arizona border, police regularly stopped cars, checked IDs, and searched for contraband. Ned was trapped. Traffic behind him wouldn't let him back up, and he couldn't make a U-turn on the narrow street. Facing up to the police was inevitable. And cops in Mexico are not like cops in the United States.

The roadblocks were officially part of a massive government crackdown on drug trafficking, but everyone in Nogales—maybe all of Mexico—knew that most of the time the cops were just looking for opportunities to shake you down for cash or iPods or cell phones or anything else they might want to keep or sell.

At least these guys were Federales, the national cops, Ned thought to himself. The state police were a lot worse. Unkempt and uneducated, those guys very rarely made any pretense about not being crooks, stealing everything that wasn't nailed down, and demanding bribes at the same time. Ned had heard the Sonora state cops were paid about $95 a week, and since expenses were about the same as they were across the border, he wasn't at all surprised they weren't exactly professional—and had their hands out at every opportunity. At least the Federales made an attempt to look like they were something more than just a gang. They almost always took bribes, but at least they usually didn't threaten you or rummage through your car for valuables.

Ned slowed and watched as the cops searched the car in front of him. He saw a few hundred pesos change hands and the pissed-off driver speed away. As the cops waved him over, Ned noticed a couple of things out of the ordinary. One of them had a goatee, which he knew was against Federale policy, and two of them were carrying AK-47 assault rifles, which he knew the Federales did not issue.

Ned had heard that members of the big drug cartels would sometimes wear police uniforms to make it easier to get away with major crimes like kidnapping and murder. He had also heard that it was them, and not the government, who really ran things in Mexico, but that they rarely bothered anyone who was not involved in the drug trade. And for the first time in his adult life, Ned was not.

He had started in high school. Fed up with authority and looking at a bleak future, Ned decided to take the easy way out. He started selling drugs, eventually becoming a full-patch member of the Sons of Satan motorcycle gang. After a huge police raid brought many of them down, Ned saved himself from a long prison sentence by ratting on his former "brothers."

The FBI put him in the witness-protection program, but he just couldn't stay away from the easy money and the adrenaline rush of crime. Some friends from work hooked him up with a branch of the Russian mafia. Ned enjoyed the work and the people, but when the stakes got too high, and he knew that some very important people wanted to see him dead, he escaped again, this time to Mexico.

A friend of a friend of a friend snuck him over the border and set him up with a job in Nogales. The city's official name was Heroica Nogales, in honor of the battles fought there, but everyone just called it Nogales. It is a big industrial city in the Mexican state of Sonora, and is almost never confused by people in the area with Nogales, the smaller agriculture-oriented city on the other side of the fence in Arizona. Ned had started to rebuild his life in Mexico. Working as an assistant manager at a screen-door factory wasn't going to make him rich, he realized, but it would keep him alive and out of prison long enough for him to make a plan.

He stopped where the cops indicated, and cranked down the window of the old Ford Tempo. "*Buenos tardes . . .* oh, hello, Gringo!" said the officer at his window. It was the guy with the goatee. Ned noticed he was wearing a lot of gold jewelry, again something the Federales discouraged if they hadn't banned it altogether. Two other cops pointed their guns at Ned, while another sat down on the sidewalk, playing a handheld video game. "You speak Spanish?"

"Pretty good," Ned answered in Spanish, and he was telling the truth. It had been his favorite subject in high school. He had picked up a lot more from the workers at the company he worked for in Delaware and he had been immersed in the language since crossing the border. He wasn't quite fluent, but certainly conversant.

"Okay, so why are you driving a car with Sonora plates?"

"It's from the factory where I work."

"Oh, you live here . . . on this side, I mean?"

"Yeah."

The cop paused and smiled. "Why?" he asked.

Ned couldn't help but laugh. So did the man questioning him. "The weather," he finally said.

"The weather is the same on the Arizona side, my blue-eyed friend."

The cop who had been playing the video game approached and interrupted. "Get him out of the car," he ordered in Spanish. This guy, taller than the others, was clearly the group's leader, despite not having any special insignia on his uniform.

Ned got out and stood in the place they motioned him to, just in front of the car. The man who had summoned him told him in English to open his mouth and show him his teeth. Then he asked, "You British?" Ned told him he wasn't. "Canadian?" Again, Ned said he wasn't. The man was clearly frustrated.

"He's not worth anything," he told the other men in Spanish and ordered them to search the car. He went back to his video game.

Since the Tempo was actually owned by the company and was used for various odd jobs and deliveries by all of the managers, there wasn't anything of value in it. On this trip, Ned was using it to pick up one of the owner's girlfriends—Lazara, an eighteen-year-old from Chiapas whose thick accent and reluctance to speak made drives with her very boring. But he certainly didn't mind ferrying around his boss's women, even Lazara, because it got him out of the factory. He hadn't seen much of Mexico, just the industrial area of Nogales where he lived and worked and a neighborhood called Colonia de Fundo Legal, where all the girlfriends lived. Neither made much of an impression on him. Most of the buildings were interchangeable—low and rectangular and either gray or beige with iron bars covering every opening. The roads were poorly paved when they were paved at all and there was litter everywhere. Dogs and small children ran all over the place, making driving a stressful nightmare. It was almost invariably sweltering and there were no trees, just small brushy bushes, dirt, rock, sand, and trash. It wasn't the Mexico Ned remembered from travel-agency ads. To him it looked more like some of the bad neighborhoods full of poured-concrete apartment blocks he had seen in Moscow, only constantly burning with heat.

The goateed cop asked him who he worked for. Ned told him, Holsamex. Radiff, an international manufacturing conglomerate based in Geneva, Switzerland, had diverse holdings around the world. One of them was Holsamex, a former warehouse in Nogales that had been converted to a factory when the North American Free Trade Agreement between Mexico, Canada, and the United States was enacted in 1994. It had originally made aluminum wheels for SUVs, but when that business went to China, Holsamex switched to screen doors.

A series of bad, often passive, decisions throughout his life had gotten Ned into such big trouble he knew he had to escape. Without taking a moment to think about it, Ned could name a number of police forces (including the FBI), two outlaw motorcycle gangs, and the Neglinnaya branch of the Russian mafia who would like to have him in their hands. The cost to save his life had been huge—just about everything he had, including his beloved vintage Indian motorcycle.

Ned's papers now identified him as Alfredo Duncan— the locals pronounced it DOON-cahn—the descendant of immigrants from South Carolina who had sought a better life in a long-forgotten Confederate colony on Mexico's Gulf coast after the South lost the Civil War.

"So . . . what do you do there?" the cop interviewing him asked.

"Assistant manager."

"Who's your boss?"

"Alvaro Fuentes Beltran."

The cop with the goatee laughed. "El Orangután? He is my cousin's cousin," he said. "Good guy, real good guy . . . don't cross him, though."

Ned smiled and agreed not only that Alvaro was a great guy (he was lying, he thought Alvaro was a pig) but also that he knew it was wise to stay on his good side. He had never heard that nickname before, but it quickly made sense. Fuentes Beltran was short and stocky with a huge potbelly and long thin arms that gave him an ape-like gait. Chronic attempts to bleach his hair blonde had left it an iridescent orange. If his situation were not so dire, Ned probably would have laughed at the idea that his boss's friends called him "the Orangutan."

When the inspection was done, the cop with the AK-47 who had been searching—clearly frustrated that he had found nothing worth stealing in the car—told Ned in Spanish that he needed "a little something" for "his time." Ned had just less than a thousand pesos on him and needed to get gas, so he handed the cop about four hundred. The man sighed and motioned for him to get back in the car.

Just as Ned turned the key, he felt a tremendous shockwave as though the car had been lifted off the ground and thrown back down again. An intense pain shot up the back of his head, and he could hear nothing but a constant screech in his ears. Outside the car he saw people running. Instinctively, he got out of the car. When he stepped out, his legs couldn't carry his weight and he stumbled to the ground. Still unable to hear, Ned looked up. Two masked men—one dressed in an army uniform and the other in jeans and a plaid shirt—were running at him. As he groggily tried to get up, each man grabbed him by one elbow and dragged him away. He passed out.

* * *

Mike Meloni knew why he was in Captain Harrison's office. As the only veteran agent at the Philadelphia FBI office who wasn't working on Operation Commando—a nationwide raid aimed at weakening MS-13, a ruthless gang from El Salvador that had set up shop in Camden, New Jersey, across the river from Philadelphia—he was going to get whatever was left over.

Harrison—one of those cookie-cutter midwestern guys with wire-framed glasses and cheap gray suits who made up the bulk of management—welcomed Meloni into his office. His reception was professionally courteous, but cold. A year earlier Meloni had discovered some local cops who were taking bribes in an investigation of crack sales in Wilkes-Barre and expanded the investigation to include them. It hadn't gained him many friends in the office, and there was a group of officers who considered him a rat—particularly one agent whose cousin was among those arrested. Besides, Meloni was from Boston's North End and had gone to MIT, a pair of facts that did not endear him to the local fraternity who took more traditional routes in their careers. Meloni didn't have many friends at the office, but—as he often reminded himself—that wasn't why he was there.

Meloni sat. Harrison sighed. "You remember Dave Kuzik?" he asked. "Must've heard he was killed in Marcus Hook?"

"Yeah," Meloni acknowledged. "Wasn't he in semi-retirement?"

Harrison gave a polite half-laugh. "Yeah, he was watching *rats*," he said, giving the word a nasty twist, "on our part of the Delmarva. And it looks like one of them had something of a problem with his management style." It was clear Harrison was playing the part of the tough, dispassionate cop while at the same time underscoring a perceived affinity between himself and the victim's possible killers. Meloni knew that Kuzik had taught Harrison a lot when he was coming up, and that he must have been upset about the murder of his old mentor. Now, in a backhanded way, the captain was letting the rat redeem himself by ferreting out the man he believed had killed a brother officer.

"It's not usually a dangerous business. In fact, I've never heard of one of those guys going down before," said Meloni, staying focused on the job at hand. "Do we have anything?"

"Yes and no," Harrison replied, with a look that told Meloni he wasn't going to do his job for him. "You'll get a complete file and all the right numbers and e-mails, but I can tell you that it was an incredibly clean job."

"Clean?" Meloni interrupted. "I heard his throat was slashed and there was blood everywhere, even a footprint."

"His throat was slashed while he sat working at his laptop . . . not the tiniest bit of struggle. It's like he didn't even know the assailant was in the room until he was already bleeding out," Harrison said angrily. "Nobody does that; makes me think this guy has military, almost certainly special forces, training."

"What about the print?"

"Commonplace Nike sneaker, men's size 12; there are literally millions of them," Harrison said with his eyebrows up. "But the impression was made some time after the time of death. Since it wasn't a robbery, it would seem as though the print were made by someone who arrived after the fact, saw the body, and fled."

Meloni paused to think about that. "And the scene? The laptop wasn't stolen or tampered with, which makes me think that neither the assailant nor the post-murder interloper were rats . . . or they were just not very smart," Meloni finished his sentence. "There's an auto-backup to the server," he pointed out, realizing halfway through his thought that Harrison was not only aware of that but would be insulted that he'd brought it up. But he continued, just as he had been taught during MIT brainstorming sessions. "Anything he had on the laptop would be in our hands already . . . although a rat probably would not know that."

Harrison did indeed look annoyed. "Yep, and you have to go through all of it—and everything else related. I want this guy caught."

Meloni thought that Harrison's dramatic tone was unnecessary, but didn't give in to the captain's desire for a fight. "Anything else I should know before I dive in?"

"Yeah, all the rats have been accounted for except one."

"Who is he?"

"A biker from the Midwest named Ned Aiken," Harrison answered. "No great shakes, caught in a roundup for traffickers, he gave up his 'brothers' in the Sons of Satan the second he could—he's a real 'great guy.'"

"Killer?"

"Just the opposite," Harrison said. "Seemed scared of the whole life; just a stupid kid who made a few bad friends and a lot of bad decisions. He could never pull off something like this."

"What about his friends?"

"What friends?" Harrison snapped. "He's a rat."

"What about rival bikers?" Meloni opined, again thinking out loud with no regard for protocol and Harrison's ego-driven give-and-take. "Some of the local guys could be impressed at how he brought down the Sons out west."

Harrison sighed and rolled his eyes. "Bikers don't work that way. It's not any enemy of my enemy—they're more like cops, a rat is a rat is a rat." He was not even attempting to hide his anger or disdain anymore. "Besides, bikers are never subtle; they never sneak up behind a guy and slit his throat; they tie him up, take him to a dump, and blast a cap in his head."

Meloni didn't let it bother him. "Suppose this guy has other friends?"

Harrison snorted derisively in what Meloni took as an attempt at laughter. "Check the file," he said dismissively. "Aiken's not just a scared rat, but let's just say he's not exactly gonna cure cancer in the next couple of days."

Meloni nodded because he knew that was what Harrison wanted. "Okay, I'll get to work on it right away," he said. "Upton will send me the stuff?"

"Yeah, her or Cervelli," Harrison answered. "Seriously, Meloni, we'll look very bad if we don't catch someone."

Meloni nodded in agreement, but his mind wasn't in Harrison's office anymore. As he got up and walked down the corridor to his own office, he had a personal brainstorming session of his own. Everybody knew Kuzik was gay, but Meloni knew that only meant trouble if he was a cruiser or a chicken hawk, and Kuzik would not have been able to hide either from the FBI unless he was way smarter than Meloni gave him credit for. Meloni's dogged adherence to thoroughness ensured he'd check it out, but it wouldn't top his agenda. It just didn't seem likely to him that Kuzik's sexuality caused or even hastened his demise.

Meloni turned his thoughts to Aiken, the guy who ran. The obvious reason to kill Kuzik would be to shut him up. And the fact that the laptop hadn't been touched did not necessarily mean it wasn't a rat . . . it could be one who was scared, or stupid. That's the kind of guy who'd see his FBI contact dead at his desk, step in a pool of blood, and then run away. It might not be what Harrison wanted, but Meloni was going to do his best to track this guy down. Even if Aiken wasn't up to killing Kuzik, he was probably the first person on the scene and that would mean he could answer a few compelling questions.

* * *

Ned woke in extreme pain. He opened his eyes to an unnatural black. A hood had been fastened to his head and his hands were tied behind his back. He was indoors and he was naked. He panicked. He tried to get to his feet and stumbled. As he came crashing down, he heard laughter. He tried again, falling to even more laughter. When he finally got up, he ran into a wall to hoots of even more, very shrill laughter.

He gave up, lying on the ground, gasping for air. He could hear more laughing. As he caught his breath, he could also hear music. His head was swimming, but it seemed as though he was at some kind of party. He could hear laughing and shouting and commotion, almost as if people were dancing. The voices seemed childish to him. And there was a repeated loud non-rhythmic thudding noise.

Finally, someone spoke to him. It sounded like a woman. "Don't feel bad, Gringo," the voice said in Spanish. "Your turn is coming next." Then Ned heard the whole room erupt into laughter. He fell still and silent. Not resigned to his fate, just unable to think of anything to help himself.

Suddenly, he heard the crash of a door and a number of men's voices shouting in Spanish. They were yelling at the partiers, asking them what they thought they were doing. Finally, Ned heard one ask, "Is that the gringo?" A sheepish, high voice answered yes, and Ned felt himself being lifted to a seated position. Someone threw a blanket on him. He felt small hands untying the hood and his hands.

The bright light hurt his eyes. As he was adjusting, somebody turned off the music. He could see the hazy image of a man in front of him. The man was ugly, with a wide, pockmarked face. He wore an expensive-looking white cowboy hat and gold chains. "Don't worry, my friend," he said in English. "We'll get you out of here, some clothes and food, you'll be fine." He and another man helped Ned to his feet. Then he yelled, "Don't make me tell Poco Loco what you did."

Ned looked around the room. It was filthy, filled with fast-food wrappers and old beer bottles. Other than the three guys who were taking him away, the other people in the room were all boys, around eleven to fourteen years old. They had a variety of weapons, ranging from baseball bats to handguns. The children were silent, looking at the floor the way guilty children do. Ned could hear some groaning, he looked back to see the fake Federale, the one with the goatee, hanging naked from a light fixture. His body was purple and bruised. He had a cloth covering his eyes. Ned could see he was trying to speak, but the man could not form his words.

Still a bit unsteady on his feet, Ned couldn't help but feel grateful to the three men who rescued him from the boys. It didn't matter to him who they were. Ned knew at his deepest level of consciousness that they were the only reason he left that room alive. As soon as the door shut behind them, he heard the music start up again.

If he was still in Nogales, he didn't know it. As he was led out the door onto the street, the sunshine temporarily blinded him. The streets were unpaved and filthy, far worse than he had seen before. Children ran everywhere, laughing at this crazy man wearing a blanket. Small dogs joined the excitement, barking and jumping to get a better look. Old people sat and stared in front of the small, cinder-block and concrete houses. This place stood in stark contrast to the old tourist hotel that had been converted to apartments for Holsamex's management staff. He had never thought of it as all that nice a place to live, but compared to this place, it was far more civilized country. As he was being led to an SUV parked out front, he could see a toothless old woman point at him and whisper something to a grizzled companion.

Though still dizzy and cloudy through the pain of his headache and shock, Ned began to assess the situation. The last thing he remembered was being questioned by Federales who did not appear to be Federales. Now he was being led from a house full of armed children into an SUV by some guys he had never seen before.

The guys were players, obviously involved with organized crime. Ned could tell from their flashy clothes, their gold, the bright white Cadillac Escalade, the way they walked, the way the kids fell silent around them and did what they were told without question. They were bad men to be sure, but they had rescued him. And years of experience had taught Ned that nobody in organized crime does you a favor unless they want something in return.

There were three of them. The man in the cowboy hat seemed to be their leader. He sat in the front passenger seat of the Cadillac. The driver was young, maybe sixteen, thin with curly hair. With his Nike hoodie, Atlanta Braves cap, and bright white sneakers, he looked like he could have walked off a street in any American town. He didn't say much, but nodded a lot. In the back seat with Ned was a behemoth, a mountain of a man, maybe three inches taller than Ned and as big around. He had huge jowls and several rolls of fat on his neck, all covered in gold chains. He was red, sweating, and panting, even though Ned had seen him exert no force other than walking from the house to the car.

They were talking in Spanish and Ned understood a great deal of it. They were joking about the guy hanging in the other room. From what they said, he was a member of a rival gang. Ned couldn't quite understand which one, because these guys kept referring to him a "Sonoran," That didn't make sense to Ned since they were in Sonora, so these men were all presumably Sonorans. He was, as Ned had already expected, a gang member masquerading as a Federale. He was, the men agreed, getting his just desserts for operating within their territory, although the fat man said that he believed nobody deserved to face those kids, who he later referred to as "little monsters."

Realizing that Ned was listening in, the boss looked at him and asked in Spanish, "How much Spanish do you know, Gringo?"

Ned blurted out "enough" realizing how stupid it sounded even before it left his mouth. Was he really trying to play the tough guy, naked except for a blanket in the back of an SUV with three presumably heavily armed men who had just saved him from a fate he could scarcely imagine? He was relieved when they laughed. He even found himself joining them.

The man in charge looked at Ned and put on a "trust me" smile, like salesmen do when they are closing a deal. "Don't worry," he said. "You'll be fine. We'll take care of you."

He knew those words were supposed to encourage him, but Ned had been around too long for them not to chill him.

* * *

For three solid days, Meloni read up on Ned Aiken, and made phone calls to verify the information in the files. Because Dave Kuzik, Aiken's contact with the agency, was dead, there was no one to elaborate on their contents.

At first glance, Aiken's story seemed spectacularly unremarkable. A high-school dropout turned biker, he turned state's witness when the heat came down. According to his own testimony, he had done well with the bikers, becoming a full patch quickly and operating his own strip joint that was also a drug distribution center.

As with every case, though, there were complications. While Aiken was in witness protection, another biker testified that he had seen him kill someone and had helped him dispose of the body. But when Meloni looked into it, he found that the witness was a drooling psycho whacked out on years and years of meth and coke abuse. After accusing his old pal of murder, the guy—Dario Lambretti—had told his doctor that they should let him go because it wasn't him that committed any crimes, that it was Duane. Duane turned out to be his cat. Although it was unlikely that talking to this wing nut would yield any answers, Meloni realized it had to be done.

He had two agents at his disposal—Javier Tovar and Carly O'Malley. Both were competent and thorough agents, but Tovar always struck him as a little more tolerant in nature, so Meloni decided to send him.

What was interesting to Meloni was how ambitious Aiken seemed to be, but also how self-defeating. He dropped out of high school, but he built a pretty impressive living as a biker and dealer. Once he sought protection, the agency put him in a menial job that he seemed unable or unwilling to do with any level of competence, but then when he assumed a management position—one that Kuzik's notes said that he found himself—he excelled, earning praise and a quick promotion. It was a legitimate job, too. Aiken had been in charge of shipping and receiving for a big air-conditioning supply factory. And Kuzik had nothing but praise for Thor Andersson, the man who owned the company.

Meloni knew that name from somewhere. He looked it up on the agency's database. Apparently, Andersson was a Swedish national who had acquired a Green card and then U.S. citizenship years ago after coming to the University of North Dakota on a hockey scholarship. He had set up shop in Delaware and had never gotten so much as a speeding ticket. But he had been questioned by the agency twice on the day Kuzik's body was found.

There had been a shooting at the Javits Convention Center on Manhattan's West Side. Two people had been killed, but the perp managed to flee. It was a heating, ventilation, and air-conditioning trade show, and Andersson had been in attendance as an exhibitor. He didn't have much to say about the shooting other than the usual "it all happened so fast" and "I couldn't tell what was happening" that a thousand other witnesses also said.

But there was one complication that set him apart from the other witnesses. During the confusion—after the shots were fired, the conventioneers stampeded like cattle—Andersson ended up with a girl. It's not that uncommon for kids to become separated from their parents when crowds got crazy, but this was different. The child didn't speak a word of English, and nobody ever stepped forward to claim her. She didn't match any file on the missing-children register. Andersson recognized that she spoke Georgian, a language that's nearly impossible to recognize unless you speak it. He claimed that although he traveled to that part of the world frequently on business, he wasn't fluent, so the Georgian consulate on 44th sent a translator to the Midtown South precinct. She told a story of coming across the ocean on a ship, meeting two men at the port and being driven around all over America on a motorcycle before ending up at the convention. The Georgian authorities couldn't find any parents for her (she claimed to be an orphan) so she stayed in the United States as the mountains of diplomatic and legal paperwork was being sorted out.

Andersson was never accused of any wrongdoing—in fact, he was praised for rescuing the girl in such a violent situation—but even he was at a loss to explain what she was doing with him. Meloni knew he had to track down the girl. Her story seemed fanciful, but it may have changed over the year since she was discovered. That thought led Meloni to look at the date. The shooting in the Javits and the discovery of the girl had happened on August 20 of the previous year. Meloni didn't have to look at the other file, but he did anyway, just to be sure. It was also the same day Kuzik's body was discovered, and the same day Aiken was last seen.

He was now sure that, in order to find out who killed Kuzik, he had to find Aiken. He would start with the girl.

* * *

The Cadillac pulled up at a ranch house outside of town. It was well maintained and large, surrounded by what had probably been farmland, but was now little more than a giant lawn of sorts. It was a dry land, and the only vegetation Ned could see for miles were small, scrubby bushes and short, hardy-looking trees. Someone had planted and maintained a few flower beds in front of the pale-blue house's large veranda, and the splash of color looked out of place in the desert.

Even more color—actually a ridiculous cavalcade of many colors—could be seen at the side of the house where a number of SUVs and customized pickup trucks were parked. When they arrived in the house's driveway, the young driver got out of the car and rummaged through the cargo area. He returned with a T-shirt, a plaid collared shirt, jeans, socks, and cowboy boots. He threw them in the back seat to Ned and told him to get dressed.

Ned put on the clothes as quickly as he could. It was awkward, changing in the back of an SUV, even a big one, and the clothes were all the wrong sizes. The shirts were too small and the jeans so huge that Ned had to hold them up with his hands. At least the boots were close to a fit.

Once outside the Cadillac, Ned followed his rescuers up to the house where they were greeted at the door by two men with assault rifles; one of them was wearing a Sonora state-police-uniform shirt and pants with cowboy boots and a baseball cap. They grinned and shot the breeze with Ned's group and the one in the uniform said something in Spanish about Ned that was just a little too quick for him to catch. All the others laughed. Ned assumed it was about his clothes.

Inside the house, Ned felt a brush of air-conditioning. In the front vestibule, a couple of chatting teenagers fell silent the moment they saw Ned's party walk through. They entered a main room, which was dominated by a group of six men playing poker. Each player had a couple of bottles of beer in front of him, and one man was smoking a cigar. Ned noticed the Cuban label that hadn't been removed. The table was littered with piles of U.S. currency, enough to buy a small house in the suburbs. There were two young women sitting on a couch behind the table. They pointed and giggled when Ned came in.

All the men started talking in Spanish. Finally, the man at the head of the table silenced them with a hand gesture. He was unremarkable looking. Short and ugly with a very prominent set of eyebrows that Ned guessed probably made him look angry even when he wasn't. He barely glanced at

Ned, instead looking at the fat man, who was panting from standing for so long. "Ratón, you know what to do," he said angrily.

The fat man then grabbed both of Ned's hands and pulled them behind his back. The other man from the car, the one in the cowboy hat, then put handcuffs on his wrists. They led him back outside and around the house into a large field. They took him to an area roughly the size of a bedroom that had been cleared of shrubbery. Beside him, he saw a freshly filled-in hole, about eight feet by eight feet. His stomach sank as he realized it was almost certainly a recently filled grave. He looked around. The fat man, El Ratón, was right behind him. With him were five other young men, one wearing a Federales uniform. They were all armed, three with assault rifles, two with handguns.

El Ratón pushed him down to his knees. One of the guys with a handgun ran in front of him and pulled out a lime-green Flip video camera and started recording. "My face isn't in the shot, is it?" asked El Ratón. The young man assured him it was not.

Then El Ratón hit Ned in the back of the head and barked: "What is your name?"

Ned answered instinctively. "Alfredo Duncan."

"Liar!" shouted El Ratón. "Who do you work for?"

"Ho-Holsamex."

"Not the DEA?"

"No, Holsamex!" Ned was shouting now, too.

El Ratón smacked him in the back of the head again. "Liar! We know how to find out the truth!" he shouted, growing hoarse. "Who do you work for? The Sonora Cartel? The Caro Quinteros?"

"No, Holsamex."

Ned could feel the barrel of a gun pressed against the back of his skull. Another interrogator had taken over from El Ratón. "We know you work for the DEA!" This new, much more malevolent-sounding voice shouted. "Just tell us you work for the DEA!"

"I don't! I don't!"

As the gun's barrel pressed deeper into the back of his skull, Ned heard a dull, electronic rendition of a popular Mexican disco song. The guy in front of him, who had been recording everything, reached in his pocket and pulled out a cell phone. He answered it, listened for a few moments, his eyes on Ned's the whole time. "Okay," he finally said. "El Orangután says he's okay. That he is for Poco Loco."

One of the men offered his hand to Ned, and helped him back to the ground. They didn't say anything to him, just led him back to the house.

Chapter Two

Driving all the way to Brooklyn with Agent Carly O'Malley was not too bad, Meloni thought to himself. Unlike most other agents, she didn't talk about much aside from what they were working on, and that was okay with him. She was very serious about her work, and he respected that. O'Malley had been something of a rising star in the agency, until a child pornography case her task force had been investigating for six months fell apart because one of her agents had gotten a bit rough with the ringleader. She took the blame and the fallout was enormous. Since then, O'Malley had been working her way back up the food chain by taking lesser assignments and working for progressively more senior agents. That she and Meloni were seen as outsiders made them natural allies, and he was relieved to be working with her, rather than having to watch his back all the time.

She was not at all unpleasant to be with on the trip, but Meloni could tell that she hated being the junior agent on any assignment. Since O'Malley never spoke with other agents about her private life, more than a few men around the office had concluded she was a lesbian; when she eventually opened up about an interest in baseball, the rumors about her spread further. Knowing she was being talked about in that way made her withdraw further, sharing even less about herself with other agents.

Meloni knew that a lot of the guys accuse any woman who isn't interested in their advances lesbians, so he didn't really give it much thought. He knew that at least one other agent had asked her out—she certainly wasn't unattractive with red hair and blue eyes—and she had shot him down. Since she knew that Meloni's interest in her was purely professional, the two of them got along well.

He was happy when she pulled out a Stieg Larsson novel and began to read, because it allowed him to go over the details of the investigation in his own head. The goal of the New York trip was to meet with the girl who turned up at the Javits the day Kuzik's body was discovered.

Hers was a complicated story. The girl, who gave her name as Sopho and her age as eleven, originally claimed to be an orphan, but later relented and told the investigators that her parents had told her that she was going to visit her rich uncle in Russia for a few weeks, and gave her to a large man with a beard to take her there. The man—who was very fat and wore a suit—drove her in a car bigger than she had ever seen to a strange and dirty town called Supsa that smelled really bad, like fire and chemicals. He gave her to another man ("he was brown like he came from India or Africa"), who put her onto a very large ship. Once aboard, she was locked in a cabin with nothing to do for a very long time. The only people she ever saw on the voyage were an old man who brought her food three times a day, and another man who brought her some water-color paints and brushes one day. Aside from that she was very bored.

When they landed, she thought she was in Russia, even though she knew you did not have to cross the sea to get there. But when she saw some black people and an American flag, she knew she had gone across the Atlantic, and it was then she became afraid that her parents had lied to her. She was given to two more men—one funny little one who was "an Arab or Turk or something" and a much bigger, more serious one who was obviously American. Neither of them spoke much of her language ("just 'hello' and 'good-bye' and things like that"), but they seemed to like her. She was shocked at how big and busy everything was. There were so many cars, she wondered if it was a holiday. While she was trying to figure out what was going on, the big man drove off with her and left the little man behind. That scared her, but she realized she had no place else to go so she stayed quiet. She stayed with the big man and they drove all over America, at first in a big shiny truck and then later on a very loud and old motorcycle. The big man took her to a huge city where there were millions of people everywhere. They went into a massive glass building, almost like a rectangular castle, that was full of people and what looked like small stores. She was in a crowd, heard some gunshots, then screaming, and saw people running. When it was all over, Andersson was holding her hand and taking her to a policeman.

Since she had refused to give the names of her parents or even what town she was from (and nobody claimed her), the Georgian embassy was at odds with what to do with her. While various American and Georgian authorities were trying to decide whose problem she was, a temporary solution was reached for her. The local Georgian consulate partnered with the New York State office of Children and Family Services and St. Nino's Georgian Orthodox Church to set her up with a Georgian American family in Bensonhurst until a permanent solution could be arranged.

As they were headed across the Verrazano Narrows Bridge from Staten Island into Brooklyn, Meloni grinned to himself at the thought that, like everyone else from Boston, he had been trained to hate everything about New York City all his life, but he just couldn't do it. He actually loved the place, the people, the food, the atmosphere, everything about it. O'Malley had emerged from her book to look around. She was originally from Long Island, so this part of the trip was very familiar to her. They had a brief conversation about the neighborhood, and O'Malley said she couldn't believe that even Bensonhurst wasn't immune to the hipster invasion that had been taking over Brooklyn.

The GPS took them into almost the center of Bensonhurst, on 79th Street near 18th Avenue. There was a high-rise apartment building on the corner, and the house they were looking for was the third of four identical red-brick row houses that looked like they were built in the 1960s.

The house looked pleasant enough, with a small, well-kept yard behind a short brick fence. Unlike many of the more elaborate houses around it, there were no crosses or icons of saints or statues of the Virgin Mary, just a simple flower garden and a small red-and-white Georgian flag sticker on the door. There was also a red-and-white van outside with the name Kwik-Key Locksmithing painted on it with a 718 phone number.

A man of about forty-five answered the door and introduced himself as Murray Khizanshvili, and told Meloni that his real name was Murtaz, but everyone in America always called him Murray. He was short and dark with a pleasant demeanor. He had a small face dominated by thick eyebrows, and he wore rimless glasses, and a big smile. Khizanshvili brought the agents into a dark but pleasant living room, made cozy by two low, brightly patterned couches. On one of them sat a woman of about forty who Meloni assumed was Murray's wife, Gvantsa, with whom he had arranged the meeting over the phone. She looked like most of the other women they had seen in the area: medium-length dark hair and a thick build, but didn't dress quite so flashily as most of her neighbors.

Beside her was Sopho, the girl they had come to see. The child in the pictures Melnoni had been given had grown up; her face and body had filled out and she looked very much like the healthy twelve-year-old she now was. Her short stringy hair had grown long and thick, and she had dyed it reddish-brown. She was wearing a bright-green, long-sleeved Abercrombie & Fitch jersey, dark jeans, and a little bit of makeup. She was polite, but neither warm nor forthcoming. After a brief discussion with the Khizanshvilis, the agents asked to be alone with Sopho. Before they could ask her any questions, she interrupted them. "First of all it's Sophia now, not Sopho," she said sternly. "And I have told you guys everything I know over and over again." Meloni was surprised at how well she spoke English after such a short time in America.

"I know," said Meloni in a way he hoped she would see as kindly. "I have the complete report right here—I have read, reread, and memorized every single word you have told the authorities."

"But we think there's more . . .," said O'Malley.

Before she could continue, Sopho shouted her down. "There isn't any more! I have told you everything!"

Meloni grinned at her. "You and I both know there's always more; like, how many eleven-year-olds don't remember their hometowns or even their last names?" he asked. After a short pause, he said, "What if I told you that nothing you tell us would be used to help send you back to Georgia?"

"Really? You promise?"

"Really," he said. "We're the FBI—we don't care where you live—we're looking for someone else."

"Who?"

"Not you," he answered. "So, can we just talk?"

"You totally promise that nothing I say will put me back in that place, with those people?"

Meloni grinned. "Totally."

She smiled nervously. "Okay, I've been lying about my parents—I know their names and where they live. I just don't want to go back."

O'Malley interjected. "I don't think you understand," she said. "We're not interested in any of that."

Sopho looked surprised. "Then what do you want to know?"

"We want to know what happened to you *after* you got off the boat," Meloni said. "About the two men who picked you up." He picked up a photograph from the file folder on his lap. "Was this one of them?"

She took the picture from him and looked at it intently and for a very long time. "Yes," she finally said. "I think he was—the tall one, the American. I think so at least."

Meloni asked her to describe her trip with him. She was hazy about much of it, but many of the details— her mention of Aiken's SUV, the motorcycle he had sold and then was accused of stealing, her description of the Hawkridge factory where Aiken had worked and to which he had taken her to steal the bike back—confirmed his suspicions. Aiken was clearly the man who picked her up, which indicated that he may have been involved in human trafficking. But a couple of things didn't make sense to him. When women are smuggled either for work or prostitution, they are usually in fairly large groups—at least a dozen. It just doesn't make any economic sense to sneak in one person. And Sopho was too young for much work and, while child prostitutes are commonly trafficked, they almost never come to the United States where cultural disdain and heavy prison sentences make it an extremely dangerous trade. The fact that no family in Georgia had emerged claiming her indicated she wasn't kidnapped for ransom or by a family member. She had said her parents had told her she was visiting an uncle, but it seemed like a story to shut her up while they were getting rid of her.

He asked her about the other man. She told him basically what she had told police and the media several times before. They had no leads on him.

"Did the two men who picked you up know the men on the ship?" he asked.

"The little one did, the big one didn't," she said. "He didn't say much of anything before the little one left."

"And did they deliver you to Mr. Andersson?"

Sopho got nervous and bit her lip. "No, I said before, Mr. Andersson had nothing to do with this, he just found me," she said. "He's a very nice man; he still visits sometimes and brings his daughters. He even bought me an iPad . . ."

O'Malley interrupted. "We know Mr. Andersson very well. We're not trying to get him into any trouble," she said. "We just want to know if the man in the picture brought you to him."

"No," she lied.

* * *

Ned was given a seat at the poker table and one of the women fetched him a cold bottle of beer. Without hesitating, he drank about half of it before setting the bottle shakily back on the table. The other men at the table laughed at him.

The ugly man who had ordered Ned's interrogation smiled at him broadly, revealing a gold tooth. "Sorry about that, my friend, but we did not know who you were," he said. "And now that we do, you are welcome to stay, but first I have to know a few things."

Fear gripped Ned's innards again. He was still in shock from his interrogation, and had no idea what was next on this group's agenda.

"First of all, we know you are not a Confederado," the ugly man said. "Those guys speak with a Veracruz accent, and you . . . well, let's just say you speak Spanish with a Kentucky accent." The men at the table laughed. One of them threw the remains of a chicken leg at Ned. "El Orangután tells me that you are an American who got into a little trouble with some bad people, and now you are in Mexico hiding from them," he continued. "Did you not realize that there are lots of bad people in Mexico, too?" His men laughed again. Ned was silent. "It's okay, man, don't worry, you're safe with us, nobody is going hurt you," the man said, then shouted at one of the women to get Ned a plate of food and another beer. "You'll stay here for a couple of days until we sort things out." He turned to the other men at the table and asked: "What should we call him?"

A brief discussion revealed that the consensus of opinion was that he was tall, white, and not very smart. One man suggested La Cigüeña (the Stork), but he was shouted down because it sounded too feminine. After much debate, they decided El Espagueti (the Spaghetti) would be more appropriate.

The ugly man laughed and shouted, "Maria, take El Espagueti to his room!"

Before he had even finished, an ordinary-looking girl of about sixteen took Ned's hand and indicated that he should follow her. She took him upstairs. Ned could hear snoring before he reached the top. The stairs led to a corridor with four doorways. At the end was a washroom, which was being cleaned by a girl about the same age as the one who was guiding him, but heavier and less pretty. On the left was a doorway with a thick dusty patterned blanket serving as a door, on the right there was a closed door and another doorway without a door. That was where the snoring he could hear was coming from.

The room was messy, but appeared as though it was cleaned regularly. A young man was sound asleep on one of the two beds, and on the floor beside him were three beer bottles and a shirt. He had attempted to get his pants off, but had only managed to get them down to his knees before giving up or passing out. He did not look to Ned to be very comfortable.

Maria motioned for him to take the other bed. Confused, Ned sat on the bed and waited for her to tell him what was going on. Instead, she started taking off her clothes. Shocked, he stopped her. "No, no, that's not what I'm here for . . ." he said.

Maria smiled. "They told me you might be a *tia*," she said, using the Spanish word for "aunt," which in Sonora was slang for a gay man. "It's okay, I should bring you up some food . . ., but I should wait a few minutes, so that they think you are a man, you know."

Ned wanted to tell her he was not gay, just scared, but he also didn't want to antagonize her or make the situation any more complicated than absolutely necessary. "What am I doing here?" he asked.

"What do you mean?" she looked confused.

"What am I doing here . . . in this room?"

"Oh, you don't understand," she smiled. "You work here now." She said, as though that would answer all his questions.

"Work? What kind of work?"

"They will tell you."

"Who will?"

"The men, downstairs," she said, getting a little frustrated with his inability to understand what to her seemed obvious.

"Yes, I know. Who are they?" Ned was getting frustrated, too, but knew he should not get her angry.

She looked at him, as though he had just asked her the stupidest question she had ever heard. "They are the men," she said. "El Apestoso is the boss here, his boss is the big boss."

Ned knew he wasn't going to get any further by questioning Maria. Instead, he smiled weakly and thanked her.

She looked at him for a few minutes and her face softened. "Here," she said. "You need this more than me." She handed him a necklace. It had a round gold charm with the face of a man with a halo and the name "Judas Tadeo" embossed on it. Ned wasn't Catholic, but he knew it was St. Jude, the patron saint of hopeless cases.

Maria went back downstairs to fetch the food and was surprised, when she returned, to find Ned sound asleep.

* * *

Meloni and O'Malley sat at a simple pine desk across from Andersson in his office at Hawkridge. Even though he was being questioned by two FBI agents about a fugitive from justice who worked for him, and a girl who was kidnapped and smuggled into the country, he betrayed not a hint of nervousness or guilt. The fugitive in question was Ned Aiken, a man he knew as Eric Steadman, the erstwhile head of his shipping and receiving department.

"I find it strange that you would hire a man like Steadman for such a senior position," said Meloni as though it was a question.

"It has always been my policy to give people chances to succeed, rather than to expect them to fail," Andersson answered. "Many people come in with résumés that are impressive, but do not strike me as smart or ambitious; Steadman did, even though his résumé was lacking."

"And how did you find him?" asked O'Malley.

"He found us," Andersson said, his eyebrows raised to indicate surprise that they would ask such a question. "This is still a small town in many ways; we do things in the old-fashioned way—I put an ad in the local newspaper, people talk about such things as a job opening."

"And you knew he was in the witness-protection program?"

"Not until after I hired him," Andersson made a show of looking at Steadman's employment file. "He mentioned in the interview that there could be complications; then one of your people, a Lieutenant Kuzik, called me and filled me in."

"And that didn't bother you?"

"Not really," he said. "The fact that he risked his life to put that sort of thing behind him actually made me a little more impressed with him."

"And how was he as an employee? Any problems?"

"Not at all, very efficient and well liked around the office," Andersson said. "As I look at his record, I can see no complaints, no disciplinary orders, and just one sick day."

"Anything suspicious about him—unexplained phone calls or visits?"

"No, nothing like that. I supplied the lieutenant with an update of his activities every two weeks," he answered. "You should have all that information."

"Now, about the little girl . . ." Meloni interrupted himself when he saw Andersson roll his eyes. "I know you have told this story a hundred times; we just need it once more."

"Yes," said O'Malley. "I'd love to hear it—just start at the beginning."

"I was in the back of our display at the Javits when I heard gunshots and screaming," he recounted. "So I ran out to see what was going on."

"Most people would have run the other way," said O'Malley.

"My military training prevented that."

"I understand," said Meloni. "You were in the special forces in Sweden?"

"Oh, no, nothing like that," Andersson laughed. "Just an ordinary foot soldier."

Meloni chuckled. "Okay, and then what happened?"

"People were screaming and running around . . . like idiots, if I may," he looked embarrassed by the frankness of his own remark. "That's when I saw Sophia—she was just standing there, obviously in shock—I was scared she was going to be trampled with all those wild people in there . . ."

"So you ran to her?"

"Yes I did."

"And you grabbed her?"

"No, I took her by the hand . . . I have children of my own, I did not want to panic her . . . If she were to run in that crowd . . . she was so small."

"You called her 'Sophia.' Didn't they tell you her name was Sopho?"

"Yes, but we have been in touch a few times since . . . thanks to St. Nino's, she asked them to contact me," he said. "She is an American girl now. She likes to be called Sophia like other American girls."

"And she went with you willingly?"

"She was in shock."

"And you knew she was Georgian how?"

"My company has been manufacturing components in various Eastern European countries for almost thirty years," he said. "I go there all the time. I know some of the languages well, but I only know a few words of Georgian. It's almost unique. I recognized it right away."

"And where did you take her?"

"Back to the display," he said. "It seemed the safest place with all the mobs at the exits."

"And then what?"

"After the SWAT team evacuated us all, I looked for a sergeant—they wear white shirts in New York City, all the other cops wear blue—and told him what had happened."

"Were you surprised to see Steadman there?" O'Malley asked.

"He was there?" Andersson looked surprised. "As I told the previous investigators, I had not seen him since the day before the convention. Are you sure he was there?"

"Yes," said O'Malley, scanning Andersson's eyes. "We have an eyewitness."

"Who?"

"You know we can't tell you that."

"Was he involved with Sophia? With the shooting? When he didn't come back to work and didn't call, I just assumed he had broken probation or something . . . you know, with the motorcycle."

"Right, the stolen motorcycle," asked O'Malley. "What do you know?"

"I didn't believe it at first, that Eric would steal his own bike," he said. "I suspected that Matt had cooked up a plot to cash in on the insurance . . . after all, Eric did sell it to him for next to nothing. When Eric didn't come back to work, I assumed he was in on it."

"An eyewitness said that Steadman had a child with him."

"I had not heard that."

O'Malley sighed and looked at Meloni. They started in on Andersson, asking him basically the same questions over again, and he answered the same each time, not wavering even the tiniest bit from his story.

After they finished with him, they used his office to question Matt, the warehouse worker who had bought the motorcycle from Ned, and Matt's wife, Katie, who had worked closely with him. Neither said they had noticed anything odd or suspicious about Ned, who they actually knew as Eric, until he sold them the motorcycle. Matt had inquired several times about buying the motorcycle—a painstakingly restored Indian—but Ned had turned him down every time. Then one night out of the blue, Ned called them and told them Matt could have the bike cheap if he just hauled it away. He had told them some story about not wanting it anymore. They didn't believe all of it, but Matt really wanted the bike, so he bought it.

Some weeks later, Matt was working in the warehouse when Esteban, one of the other warehouse guys, came running in shouting that someone was stealing his bike. Matt hadn't been able to see who had taken it, but he was pretty sure it was Eric because he never saw him again after that. Eric was one of the few people who knew how to start the thing and, as its former owner, it made sense that he would have a spare set of keys.

Meloni and O'Malley then interviewed Esteban, who was worried that he might be deported back to El Salvador. Meloni assured him repeatedly that he wouldn't be, that all they were interested in was what he saw on the day the motorcycle was stolen. It took a while, but Esteban eventually revealed that he saw a man and what could have been a little girl or a boy get on the Indian. He had seen them when he heard the man begin to kick-start the big machine.

He knew it was Matt's bike. It was all Matt had talked about for weeks. He wasn't sure if the man was Eric or not. Eric had worked upstairs and rarely came down to the warehouse. The thief had looked a bit like Eric, but Esteban had only seen him from behind and from a distance, so he wasn't sure.

After they excused him, Meloni asked O'Malley if she thought Aiken was the man who had stolen the bike. "At the risk of jumping to conclusions," she answered, "yes."

* * *

Nina, a Russian model who had once befriended Ned, was grilling sturgeon and lobsters on their friend Viktor's yacht . . .

"Wake up, sleeping beauty!"

Ned's eyes sprung open. A short, stocky man wearing a red western shirt and jeans, and carrying an AK-47, was kicking his bed.

"Come on, downstairs," he ordered, and waited until Ned went in front of him before leaving the room.

In the main room, he saw three men at the table. El Ratón, the obese man who had interrogated him; beside him was the guy he saw passed out the night before; and on the other side of the table sat a man Ned did not recognize. He was smaller and darker and dressed differently than the other Mexicans he had seen in Nogales. His clothes looked homemade and simple. They fell silent as they saw Ned enter the room.

"Ah, El Espagueti! My best gringo friend," El Ratón said in what seemed like a friendly way, but still sent chills. "Don't be sensitive, my friend. You are obviously a man of the world. You must know that we have to protect ourselves."

Ned understood the group's need to protect itself, but did not know who they were. Even though he had been in Mexico for a while, he had tried to lay low and his knowledge of organized crime in the country was limited. His first experience of criminal gangs was his involvement with and eventual membership in the Sons of Satan Motorcycle Club in the States. At first, he thought bikers were just guys who rode Harleys, smoked weed, and generally had a good time together. But he soon learned that the gang was a cutthroat corporation based on drug and human trafficking, and that the penalty for failure or disloyalty was death.

He took a moment to piece together what had happened and how he had gotten there. The "Federales" who had originally stopped him were clearly working for one of the cartels. Realizing he was of little value, they were letting him go when he was attacked and caught in the crossfire. As far as the explosion was concerned, Ned attributed it to a car bomb or a rock-propelled grenade, both of which were in common use by the cartels.

Ned also knew that the big cartels often increased their manpower by kidnapping people off the streets, but wondered why they wanted him in particular. Perhaps, he thought, somebody knew who he was. And it suddenly dawned on him that he had been working in association with the cartels for years.

The bikers bought drugs, mainly cocaine, wholesale from the Italians and then sold them to street-level dealers to retail. He never really thought about where the drugs came from before the Italians had them, but he had guessed Colombia or Bolivia.

Later, he had become mixed up with the Russian mafia and learned that they got drugs from terrible, war-torn places like Afghanistan and Chechnya and sold them around the world. The Russians were far more sinister, capable of far worse horrors than any biker gang.

But Ned never really thought that much about Mexico. Like many Americans, he always considered Mexico just a slightly rougher version of his own country. He associated it with weed because of movies and TV and because all the Mexicans he knew were big pot smokers. But he also knew from experience that there's no real profit in pot. Sure, for a small operator it can make a few bucks, but because it sold so cheaply—everyone seemed to be growing the stuff—it was generally for small-timers.

These guys were anything but small-time. They had expensive weapons and they used methods—like bombings and impersonating cops—that most bikers could only dream about and the Russians didn't have to bother with. It was a sophisticated operation, even if all the guys running it seemed a bit sloppy.

All of that ran through his head in the second or so between what El Ratón said to him and his response. "I understand."

"Good—Jessica! Go get him breakfast—please sit down," the big man said, motioning for him to take a chair beside the little guy in homemade clothes. As he got closer, Ned was shocked by how small the man was. "El Espagueti, this is El Chango," he gestured to the little guy, whom he had just called "the Monkey." Then he pointed to the other man. "And you know El Vaquero Loco from upstairs." Ned didn't know which of the company El Ratón was referring to, but assumed he was the one who'd been passed out on the bed. Aside from El Ratón, who looked a little like a Mexican version of Biggie Smalls, he couldn't have picked any of these men out of a police line.

Once Ned was seated, Jessica, a teenager like Maria, put a plate of scrambled eggs, dark-red sausages, and some pickled peppers in front of him, along with a cup of hot, black coffee. "El Vaquero Loco is your teacher now," El Ratón instructed, his jowls vibrating wildly as he spoke. "Do everything he says."

El Chango said something very quickly in thick, accented Spanish; Ned could hardly make it out. "Fucking *mara*! Sometimes I think everyone from Guatemala is fucking retarded!" El Ratón shouted. "You never ask who the boss is! El Vaquero Loco is your teacher; you do what he says, that is all you need to know." El Chango flinched visibly.

El Ratón reached for a knapsack that was on the table. From it, he pulled out three pairs of cell phones and handed one of each pair to both El Chango and Ned. "The smart phone, the LG, is a bluff," he instructed. "If anyone demands your phone, like a soldier or a Federale, you give him this. Save some numbers on it to make it look real." Then he grabbed another, bigger phone with a small keyboard from Ned's pile. "This, the BlackBerry, you hide," he said. "It is also a bluff, it is in case you get searched—it is full of fake numbers. The cop will think the first was a decoy and this is your real phone." Then he picked up an older-looking phone, one that folds in half. "This one, the Nokia, is your real phone," he said with a smile. "It has only one number on it and will only ever have one number on it. That number is El Vaquero Loco's—he is the only person you will ever call on this phone. Heaven help you if I ever see another number on this phone." Ned thought that the idea of using the newer, more sophisticated phones to mislead police was pretty astute.

El Ratón then put his huge paw back in the knapsack. "These are the SIM cards," he said, handing them little plastic rectangles. "The phones won't work without them. Put them in the phones when you use them, and take them out of the phone when you are finished. Do not leave the

SIM card in the phone. Heaven help you if I find a SIM card in your phone. Nobody will ever call you, so you don't need it."

He put his hands back in the knapsack and withdrew two handguns. They were cheap looking, obvious copies of better-known guns, and clearly made to poor standards. The colors of their components didn't quite match and there was even a small metal burr clinging to the cocking mechanism of one of them. El Ratón handed them each one. "These are for now," he said. "You won't need them, but just in case. Now, like I told you, El Vaquero Loco is your teacher; do what he says and everything will be fine. Don't do what he says and you will be in trouble. Simple, even for you, *mara*."

El Ratón got up and waddled his way out of the house. El Vaquero Loco, who had been quiet up to this point, spoke to the two new surprised recruits. "You heard the big man, you do what I say now," he smiled. The look of utter delight on his face made Ned's stomach turn. He'd seen it before. Experience had taught him that the more someone wants power, the more likely they are to want to put it into action. El Vaquero Loco looked very much like he was going to be a pain in the ass, at the very least.

El Chango asked him something Ned could just barely understand. El Vaquero Loco replied, "Not now, El Chango. Eat your breakfast, have a beer, play some poker. I'll tell you when I need you. Until then, you are free to just hang around."

Chapter Three

Ned was not sure what to do. After El Vaquero Loco left, he sat at the table with El Chango while about a dozen or so armed men milled around the house, both inside and out. He knew that he was not quite free to go, but he also knew that the men had no interest in harming him—at least for now. They clearly had plans for him. He hadn't been kidnapped—there was nobody to ask to pay a ransom for him—but he was being held. The feeling he had was very much like that he had after he was arrested—a mixture of dread, anticipation, and uncertainty.

He wondered about El Chango, why they had held him as well. Ned knew he had some value to these guys—even if he didn't know exactly what it was—but he couldn't see any reason to hold this little guy who looked like he just walked off a documentary about Third-World farming. As Ned caught his eye, the smaller man started talking so quickly that Ned could hardly tell if he was speaking Spanish. Ned smiled, and asked El Chango to slow down so that he could understand him, explaining that Spanish was not his first language.

El Chango smiled. "Not mine, either," he said.

"I thought El Ratón said you were from Guatemala. Don't they speak Spanish there?"

"Lots of people do, but I'm from way out in the country," El Chango told him. "I speak Q'eqchi'—you know, Mayan."

"Mayan? Like those guys from hundreds of years ago?" Ned had vague memories from history class, of temples and human sacrifices, running through his head.

"We're still here."

Ned looked to see if El Chango was offended by what he'd said, but he didn't seem to be. He had a broad, innocent-looking face that looked like it had no choice but to telegraph his emotions. El Chango did not look like the Mexicans Ned had seen. He was smaller, darker, and had an altogether different—almost Asian—look about him. Right now, though, he looked frightened; the pained expression on his face indicated he was in a stressful, but somehow familiar, situation.

"What about you, *canche*?" he asked. "What are you doing here?"

"*Canche*?"

"You know, 'blondie,' like how the Mexicans say *guero*," El Chango smiled sardonically. "It's what we call white people back home."

Ned had been lying about his identity and his past for so long, he didn't have an immediate answer. He wondered what he should tell El Chango. Then he let his mind run wild with paranoid thoughts. Was this little man being paid by the FBI? The bikers? The Russians? Years of running had taught Ned that the less people knew about him, the safer he was. As innocent as this little man looked, Ned knew better than to trust him. All he said was: "Same as you."

El Chango laughed childishly. "I doubt that," he said. Then he told Ned his own story, about how he had a cousin who was one of a large group of Guatemalans who had made it to the United States a year earlier. Ned could not make out every detail as El Chango would sometimes speak too quickly or in dialect, but he was able to follow the overall plot. El Chango's cousin and some other Guatemalans had gotten jobs at a pork slaughterhouse and meat-packing plant in Wapello County, Iowa. He couldn't believe it when he heard that the Americans didn't want to work, that they would refuse to do an honest day's work for the kind of money very few Guatemalans had a chance to make. The place was strange to him at first—he experienced things like constant electricity and indoor plumbing at home for the first time—but he soon grew to love the place. He had money and friends. The winters were cold, terribly cold, but the rest of the time, it was really a wonderful place to live.

El Chango—who said his real name was Maguin Avi Menchú—decided he would go to Iowa, meet up with his cousin, work at the plant, save up a lot of money, and return to Guatemala and buy a house and a car. He and about a dozen other people from his hometown, La Reinita in Sayaxché province, sold everything they had and took buses to the Mexican border. The Mexican border guards, he said, hated when Guatemalans snuck over the border, and could even be dangerous sometimes, but a couple of bribes lubricated their passage. Once inside Mexico, the group traveled north, either walking, hitchhiking, or taking buses when they could. Sometimes they would work on farms for a little extra cash or just for food and a safe place to sleep.

The trip was a revelation to El Chango. He had no idea Mexico was so big or so diverse. In the south, it was a lot like Guatemala with jungles, farms, and friendly people. But then it gets dry and mountainous and the people are busy, arrogant, and rude. There are cities everywhere with unbelievable traffic and so many huge buildings. Smoke is everywhere and the Guatemalans often found themselves coughing and wheezing. After that, it becomes a terrible desert with no water, no trees. And the people are different, bigger, and they dress funny, in jeans and boots. They almost never speak and are very aggressive, almost like they are angry all the time. The Guatemalans found them strange and even a little bit frightening.

The little group made it to Nogales and, as soon as they were within an hour's walk of the border, they met the "coyotes." Ned was familiar with coyotes, professional border crossers, from his own experience sneaking into Mexico. But things were different for El Chango. While Ned's coyotes worked in total secrecy, meeting with go-betweens in dark bars north of the border, they are very open in Mexico. As El Chango and the other Guatemalans walked through the city, men in pickup trucks and vans would shout at them, telling them they would get them over the border, quoting prices, and with each claiming their service was the best in town.

Confused, the group's leader—a man named Gaspar Huerta—decided to go with the coyote who had the biggest truck. The man they picked also looked to be the richest of all the coyotes they had seen, which made them think that he knew what he was doing. But instead of taking them to the border, the man took them to a ranch outside the city. It was full of armed men who took everything they had and separated them from each other. El Chango didn't know what had happened to his friends, just that he was taken to this house the same day as Ned and told he was going to work, but nobody explained what that work was. Because they had given him a gun, he was scared about what that work might be.

Ned agreed that the men they were with were criminals, and that no matter what they planned for them, it was almost certain to be very dangerous.

* * *

Even though he had tried to prepare himself, Agent Tovar still couldn't help but laugh a little inside when he stepped off the plane in Minneapolis. He had long wondered if the people there really would sound like the characters on *Fargo*, and when they actually did, he was delighted.

He knew it was wrong to mock people, even to himself, so he just thought of it as enjoying their regional eccentricities. A native of Brownsville, Texas, he had long found the Philadelphia accent funny, but the Minnesotans really put them to shame. Though most of the agents at the office were tough or dour, using only gallows humor and pranks to break the tension, Tovar was different, almost an oddity in his ability to stay detached. That quality endeared him to Meloni as much as it unnerved other agents. And in that way that was typically Tovar's, he was thinking not about the case, but whether or not he could sweet-talk his way into a free rental-car upgrade.

Things got more serious when he arrived at the hospital to interview Dario Lambretti. Chedoke House seemed like any kind of normal outpatient facility, except for the high, razor-wire-topped fence and guard towers. Once he was past the front security desk, a uniformed and armed guard took him through the halls on his way to the interview room. Throughout the center, men who he took to be patients milled about in comfortable clothes, and a few uniformed orderlies—who he noted were all Hispanic— quietly attended to their tasks. By institutional standards, the place seemed tranquil, even comfortable, with not much of the tension and coldness one feels when visiting a prison. It really did feel to him like a place of rehabilitation, not incarceration.

The guards led Tovar to what looked like a very ordinary corporate conference room with no windows. Inside was a morose-looking man with round horn-rimmed glasses and very short hair. He barely acknowledged Tovar as he entered. Tovar knew it was Dr. Hesse-Grimwald, the man he had spoken with on the phone. Hesse-Grimwald was an expert on drug-induced psychosis and was a leading voice in experimental rehabilitation methods. When he finally looked up from the papers he was reading, he glared at Tovar from over his glasses. "You know that Lambretti is a very advanced case, don't you?" he said with an accusatory tone. "He has been put through questioning dozens of times, and nothing he has ever said has stood up in court. I can't see why you would want to talk to him at all."

Tovar sighed. He told the doctor he understood, that he had a cousin, a close one, about his age who was a heroin addict.

"They are not the same," the doctor snapped. "Heroin is a narcotic. Meth is a stimulant. They are completely different. They have different effects on the mind and body. If you are not the right man for this . . ."

Tovar assured him he was. The doctor reluctantly picked up the receiver of the phone in the middle of the table. "Geraldo, send him in."

Two orderlies escorted a man in jeans and a denim shirt into the room. He was thin and spent-looking, but nowhere near as badly off as the toothless, hollow-cheeked pictures Tovar had seen of him. There was a vacant appearance in his eyes and he had a tendency to fiddle with things, but otherwise Lambretti looked very much like someone you'd encounter on the street and barely notice. The agent shook his bony, unsure hand and made some ineffective small talk about the weather. Sensing that the two men were eager to get the whole interview over with as quickly as possible, Tovar stormed right in. "How do you know Ned Aiken?"

"Sons of Satan back in Springfield. I was a full patch and I was told to look after him and another kid," Lambretti recalled. "The other guy was an idiot, but Crash Aiken was a good kid."

"Really? Did he ever get into trouble?"

Lambretti smiled, but it betrayed no happiness or mirth. "If I had a dollar for every time," he sighed, "I'd probably buy some more meth." Then he laughed. "Like I told you guys, I saw him kill a guy—it was an accident, really, a fight that got out of hand—and I helped him get rid of the body." He made a splashing noise and gestured with his hands. "It's at the bottom of Springfield Harbor . . . or at least it was. Those suckers and bottom-feeders will tear you up pretty good."

They discussed the circumstances of the death, which seemed entirely plausible to Tovar, as did the breakdown and ultimate disposal of the body. Lambretti said he did not know the victim's identity, nor could he put specific details together like time or date. They also talked about the raid that took them all down, but Lambretti apologized for not being able to remember large chunks of what had happened.

"Tell me about Ned Aiken."

"What, as a person? As a biker?" it was clear Lambretti was trying to recall everything. Hesse-Grimwald had told Tovar that it was part of Lambretti's therapy to recall as much as he could about his past truthfully. "Some of the guys thought he was stupid, but he wasn't really. He was just unsure of how to go about things. Ned was brought in by his uncle—who was something of a fuck-up in his own right—and when he was offed right away, everybody wanted a piece of Crash. He worked hard, but always seemed a bit, you know, ill at ease."

They spoke for about a half-hour about various aspects of Ned's life and character. Tovar asked the same questions over again and crossed a few over to see if the overlapping answers checked out. Everything Lambretti told him jibed with what he already knew. Lambretti apologized frequently for having holes in his memory, and Tovar assured him it was okay.

By the time they were through, Tovar assembled a pretty well-defined picture of Aiken's character. He seemed something of a babe in the woods, naturally intelligent, but unschooled in the ways of the world and especially crime. He seemed a passive character, but in possession of a survival instinct a rat would envy.

* * *

Ned and El Chango were sitting together on the ranch house's front porch nervously waiting for a sign they had not been forgotten about. Ned guessed it was close to noon when three casually dressed young men headed in their direction. One of them, taller than usual for the area but still shorter than Ned, approached them. He was wearing sunglasses with mirrored lenses. "Gringo, Chango, you are coming with us," he ordered them. "He led them to a giant

Chevy Suburban SUV. It was bright white with blacked-out windows and elaborate pinstripe decals. Ned could hear heavily synthesized Ranchera music from inside before he they even opened the doors.

El Vaquero Loco was sitting in the third row of seats. One of the men who had brought them to this place joined him. Ned and El Chango were instructed to take the second row, while the tall man took the seat next to the driver, the youngest man of the group, who turned down the volume on the stereo. El Vaquero cleared his throat and then made an announcement. "Today is your first day on the job," he said pompously. "What I see today can have lasting effects on your future. Be smart, do what we say and you could become very, very rich. Otherwise, things will not go so good for you."

The other men in the SUV began to laugh. Ned noticed that they were taking dirt roads from the ranch, but the area around them was growing increasingly populated. He tensed up when he saw a state police checkpoint at a bustling country crossroad, and he was surprised to see the big, ostentatious car simply waved through.

The man in the sunglasses spoke to them as though nothing had happened. "Your job today is to make some deliveries," he said. "Take a small package to who we tell you and get a small package back—very simple, even for you, El Chango!"

Everyone in the car laughed, expect Ned and El Chango. Ned looked over at him, in part to judge what his own reaction should look like. El Chango did not look good. He was staring intently at nothing. There were beads of sweat on his face even though the air-conditioning had cooled the inside of the big truck. He was visibly shaking when the Suburban stopped at the next intersection.

Ned looked around outside. The Suburban had stopped at a roadside melon stand. From his own experience, Ned knew that many people in Sonora really value farm-fresh food, and he had come to enjoy it as well. Watermelons were particularly appreciated in the hot, desert region. There were three men at the stand. Two were sitting, and the other had approached the SUV to speak with the man in the front passenger seat.

As the window rolled down, El Chango pulled his hand-gun from under his seat and pointed it at the head of the tall man in the front seat. He squeezed the trigger. Nothing but the tap of metal on metal. He swung the gun around and aimed at the driver. He pulled again with the same result. Realizing that his gun wasn't loaded, El Chango dropped it, opened his door and ran, stumbling when he hit the ground.

The driver and the tall one quickly ran after him. The melon-stand guys ran in the other direction. Since both sides of the road were bounded by steep, scrub-covered hills, El Chango had no choice but to run along the road the way that they had come. His pursuers bounded after him. Suddenly, the driver stopped, raised a handgun, and fired. He missed. El Chango ran more frantically, with his hands on the back of his head. The tall character stopped running and fired. El Chango fell to the ground. As he was stumbling back to his feet, he was hit again. Ned could see from how his neck snapped that it was a headshot and realized that El Chango was not going to get up ever again.

The driver turned and returned to the car. He stuck his head in El Chango's still-open door and asked El Vaquero Loco what he should do with the body. "Leave it there, put a sign on it," his boss ordered in an annoyed tone. "And close the fucking door, the noise is bothering me."

The driver then opened the truck's tailgate, and took out a bright green sheet of cardboard, some string, and a Sharpie. He wrote something on the cardboard, then took it over to El Chango's body and tied it to his finger.

As he was returning, the two men in the backseat were joking about how stupid Mayans were and how El Vaquero Loco had bet the other guy that El Chango would never work out and that he now owed him 100 pesos. When the other two men were back in the car and the laughter died down, El Vaquero Loco asked Ned: "Okay, El Espagueti, what did El Chango do wrong?" All the men laughed again.

Ned did his best to grin. "He did not do what you said for him to do."

El Vaquero Loco grinned widely. "Yes, that is exactly right." They sped off for Nogales. The guys in the front seat waved as they passed by the out-of-breath watermelon salesmen, sitting by the side of the road.

* * *

Meloni had called O'Malley and Tovar in for a discussion about the state of the case. He had read their reports from their respective trips and other investigations and wanted to brainstorm before making his next move. He especially wanted to hear from O'Malley. She had not told him anything about her recent investigations into Aiken's and Andersson's pasts. It was almost like, he feared, she was conducting a separate investigation. Over coffee and biscotti, they discussed what they already knew. Meloni opened the session. "So what do we know about Ned Aiken?"

"Not a whole hell of a lot," said O'Malley. Meloni wondered if she was withholding information.

"Oh, come on," Meloni encouraged. "We know he joined the Sons and bailed on them after the raid. We know he had a terrible job and was useless at it. We also know he found his own job, a better job, and did quite well. What about his boss, Andersson?"

"Andersson's story totally checks out," said Tovar, oblivious of the tension between the other two officers. "State department, local cops, immigration, I have been back and forth over this guy's records and there is nothing to indicate he has done anything wrong."

O'Malley smirked. "Except that he just happened to employ a guy who disappeared the same day his agency contact was murdered, watched two people get murdered at a conference, and took possession of a small child that we were told had been in company with our missing perp."

"Suspect," Meloni corrected. "But you are right, Andersson can't be as clean as his record indicates—it's impossible to do big business in Eastern Europe without some connections. He's smart, but I'm sure something will come out if we look under enough rocks."

"Yeah, and Sophia didn't instill me with a ton of confidence on that front, either," O'Malley answered. "I could see Aiken wanting to give her to Andersson—he's a family man with good standing in the community—if he cared about the girl at all, he would know to drop her with the boss."

"Indeed, but why would Ailken care about the girl? How did he come in contact with her in the first place?" Tovar interjected. "It's clear she was being sent over here against her will . . ."

"But why?"

"Lots of perverts out there," Meloni said with a quick glance at O'Malley. "You should know that better than either of us."

O'Malley was angry that her new boss would bring up her bungled child porn case. "Okay, let's say that's why she was kidnapped and smuggled," she said, trying not to sound annoyed. "What would Aiken be doing with that element—he's a Midwestern biker not an international man of mystery."

"A former Midwestern biker who just happened to work in shipping and receiving for a company that contracts work all over Eastern Europe," Meloni pointed out. "He had almost unlimited access to bad guys when you really think about it—anyone could have made him an offer."

Tovar agreed. "He certainly was ambitious," he said. "Raced through the ranks of the Sons in record time then re-established himself in the legit world, without our help, while under protection."

O'Malley snorted. "Maybe we gave him too much help."

After a brief discussion about who Ned knew and how, Meloni brought up the key piece of evidence he thought could connect all the threads together—the Indian.

O'Malley agreed. "Bikers often love their bikes, and he put a lot of money and effort into that one."

"But he gave it up the second he got a luxury car," Tovar pointed out.

"And stole it back soon thereafter," O'Malley one-upped him.

"Yeah, not the brightest plan," Tovar said. "Not many people can even start, let alone ride, one of those things, so he very likely did steal it. If he still had the key, why did he get rid of it in the first place?"

Meloni agreed. "And the bike was ancient. Those things always need parts—Tovar, can you track down all the Indian parts wholesalers and retailers, see if anyone has bought anything for that particular make and model?" Tovar agreed.

"You're right," O'Malley said. "He is an idiot. Keep in mind that he's the guy who tried to flee into Canada in a rental car. With a woman."

That comment struck Meloni with another possible line of inquiry. He had forgotten about Aiken's attempted escape into Canada. And he had forgotten about the woman. Ned wasn't alone in that rental car. After questioning she'd been deported to some obscure Eastern European country . . . he tried hard to think of the name. He had to track her down. He'd put Tovar on it because of his experience with international investigations. O'Malley would look for the bike.

* * *

At the edge of the city, the Suburban pulled into a Pemex gas station. Pemex was the government-run petroleum company and their green-and-red filling stations were everywhere in Mexico. Ned instinctively glanced at the car's gas gauge, it was three-quarters full.

El Vaquero Loco handed Ned a small paper bag. "Here, take this to the man inside; make sure you give it to Ivan, not Pedro," he told him. "You, Guason, go with him." The guy in the front passenger seat, the tall one who had shot El Chango, nodded and got out of the car. Ned idly wondered why his nickname was regional slang for "lazy." As instructed, Ned got out of the car and walked with Guason to the gas station's store.

Inside there were two men: one sitting and reading a magazine, the other manning the cash register. Guason slapped Ned on the back and told him to get on with it. Ned looked at the man behind the till, whose left hand was missing, and asked if he was Ivan. The man just sighed, raised his good hand and pointed at the man with the magazine. Ivan looked up from his magazine and asked Ned what he wanted. Ned handed him the bag. Ivan looked surprised, and looked inside the bag. He made a questioning look at Ned and looked like he was about to speak when he caught sight of El Guason. He then smiled and nodded. He took the paper bag into a back room with a door marked "Employees Only," returned with a plastic shopping bag full of Mexican currency, and handed it to Ned. Ned thanked him and Ivan laughed. Pedro sighed.

Ned and El Guason left the little store and started toward the Suburban. El Guason spotted a pair of cops sitting in a bright white Sonora state police car behind the Suburban and, to Ned's utter confusion, walked over to them, motioning Ned to come with him. The plastic shopping bag was translucent and stuffed with cash. There was no way Ned could hide it. "Hello, officers," El Guason said to the cop on the passenger side. "You know why I like a fat cop?"

The officer, who was pretty heavy, was angered and obviously insulted but also intimidated, and just grunted. El Guason answered anyway. "Because he's always hungry and he can't chase you," he said. "Espagueti, give these nice officers something for their time." Ned didn't know exactly how much money he was supposed to give the cops, so he just pulled a bill out of the bag. It was a 500-peso note. He handed it directly to the fat cop who just nodded.

Once inside the Suburban, Ned noticed the police car pull away. "He was okay," El Guason told El Vaquero Loco. "He was calm, handed the product over, took the cash, didn't freak out."

"How much did you give *la chonta*?" El Vaquero Loco was addressing Ned directly. He used a slang term for cops that translated literally to "wanker" that was not common in Sonora, but Ned understood it anyway.

"Five hundred."

"For both?" El Vaquero Loco smiled broadly. "Espagueti, you are a natural." The men in the car laughed. El Vaquero Loco told him they would have a party when they got back to the ranch. "Just a few more stops," he assured him. "Now that you know how things work, you can do this by yourself—make lots of money." Ned tried his best to smile.

"Don't worry, my gringo friend," El Guason said. "You are one of us now—you are safe." Ned only felt more frightened.

* * *

O'Malley came into Meloni's cubicle and threw down a file folder. "I have a small amount of good news and a great deal of bad news," she told him.

Meloni rolled his eyes and sighed. "The good news is?"

"I tracked down the file on the woman who was with Aiken when he tried to flee the country," she answered. "Her name is Daniela Eminescu and she's a Moldovan national, since deported."

"And we know where she is?"

"That's the bad news," O'Malley said. "We don't. Moldova is one of the poorest and worst-run countries in Europe, a very easy place to disappear into."

"We have people there?"

"No, but the CIA has plenty—just look at the location, it's Moldova, a former Soviet republic," she replied. "And there's Interpol."

"And the locals?"

"Bad news—considered among the worst police forces in all of Europe, if not *the* worst," she said. "You name the type of corruption and they have it—torture, bribery, links to organized crime, links to terrorism, missing suspects, everything they can do, they do."

"And even if we find this woman, what are the chances she'll tell us anything of value?" His experiences with questioning girlfriends and ex-girlfriends had left him less than ambitious at the prospect of getting much out of this one. It would be different if he had something to offer her, but couldn't think of anything.

"I thought you told us to exhaust every lead," said O'Malley, reminding Meloni that she was just as capable of taking over as he was.

* * *

The following day, Ned was sitting in his room. He had woken up at about six in the morning and could not get back to sleep. He was alone in the big room, and it did not make him any more comfortable. He could hear noise from downstairs—it actually sounded like a party—and did not want to leave the room. Instead he waited, trying to formulate a plan. If he could manage to escape, where would he go? All of these guys were friends of his boss over at Holsamex, and he really didn't know anyone in the country who was not attached to the company. He could try to make it back across the border, but even if he succeeded, he would be taking his chances with the FBI, the Russians, and the bikers. Unable to figure out a way out, he defaulted to laying low, doing what the men who were holding him instructed and getting out when he could get his hands on some real cash.

As he was thinking to himself, Ned was startled by El Guason, who stumbled in the door, blind drunk. He staggered to the bed El Vaquero Loco had been in the night before and wriggled around, trying to get comfortable. On his back, he turned his head to face Ned and grinned. He spoke to him in Spanish. "Ah, gringo, *guero*, you should not be so scared," he said. "It's a good life . . . cars, money, guns, women, drugs . . . anything you want. All you have to do is, like you say, play ball."

Ned did his best to smile and nodded.

"No man, you don't understand," El Guason said. "You are one of us now, and we are going to be in charge very, very soon."

"In charge . . . of what?"

"This place, Sonora," El Guason looked at Ned as though he was incredibly stupid. "The local guys are such cowards—they look tough, these cowboys, but they run when they see us." He grinned.

"What about the cops? The government?"

El Guason laughed. "We own the cops," he said condescendingly. "And we are the government. We have nothing to worry about."

Ned wanted to ask him what he meant by that, but El Guason was snoring even before he finished his sentence.

Chapter Four

The sounds coming from downstairs died down at about seven-thirty in the morning. The music stopped, the laughing and talking finished, and Ned heard the front door open and close a number of times. Hungry, curious, and urgently needing to use the washroom, Ned emerged from his bedroom, passing the loudly snoring El Guason on the way. The washroom was at the end of the hall, and he had to step over a passed-out man to get inside.

Once finished, and grateful that Jessica, Maria, and the others were around to clean up after these men, Ned headed downstairs. He hadn't heard anyone speak or do anything other than snore for about a half-hour, so he felt bold enough to explore his surroundings.

The living room was dominated by the sight and sound of El Ratón, who was sound asleep on his back at the bottom of the stairs. The noise coming from him sounded to Ned like it came from a poorly maintained chainsaw. Ned marveled at how big the man really was. He was under so much more duress when they had been together earlier that Ned failed to really comprehend his enormity. Though not very tall, Ned estimated his weight as close to, if not exceeding, 400 pounds. The girls had not cleaned the area around him yet.

That presented a major problem for Ned. Although he wasn't exactly committed to a serious escape attempt from the ranch house, he also knew it was not in his best interest to wake anyone either. They were all armed, presumably still drunk, and not the type of guys you'd want to wake with a start. Ned took his shoes off and held them in his left hand. Using his right hand on the stair railing to steady himself, he leapt over El Ratón. He succeeded in clearing the big man, but also knocked over two empty Coors Light bottles. Terrified that the sound of the clattering bottles would awaken at least some of the men in the room, Ned dove behind a door into the dining room. There were more sleeping men in there. Despite the noise, nobody even stirred.

With a chuckle to himself, Ned put his shoes back on. He walked out the front door and stood on the edge of the veranda. The ranch was huge. There weren't any cattle anymore, but the scrub was low and sparse, as it was over all the flat parts of Sonora that were not actively irrigated. There was one well-rutted dirt road out of the front gate, but the fence around the whole ranch was small and in ill repair. If he had somewhere to go, Ned thought to himself, it would not be too hard to get out of here.

As he pondered his immediate future, Ned was startled by the sound of metal clamping onto metal. He spun around and saw a man sitting in a chair, holding an AK-47. The man, who had long hair, a small beard, purple-tinted sunglasses, and a long, buttery-looking leather jacket laughed. "Sorry to scare you, man," he said in English. "Go back to what you were thinking about. I have to finish cleaning Rosalita." The man took a moment to apply oil to a cloth that he then used to polish the gun. Ned was not just surprised that the man spoke English, but that he would engage him in conversation. Everyone else at the house had been tight-lipped except to curse him, mock him, or bark out orders. In fact, Ned was cautiously relieved to have someone to talk to.

Ned was at a loss. He felt like it would be appropriate to introduce himself, but he wasn't ready to reveal his identity any more than he had to. Looking for something to say, he blurted out "nice gun."

The man laughed. "It is, it is," he grinned. "You have one, a *cuerno de chivo*?"

Ned was confused. *Cuerno de chivo* meant "goat's horn" in Spanish. "Say what?" he asked.

"Wow, you really are new to Mexico," the man laughed. "*Cuerno de chivo* is what we call the AK-47 here, the magazine, the clip, you see here, is curved like a goat's horn. Many Americans say it looks like a banana, but we prefer to say goat's horn—a little more poetic. Would you like to hold her?"

Surprised at the offer but not wanting to offend, Ned said he would, and the man handed it to him. In an instant, images of himself killing the man and shooting his way out of captivity rushed through his head. But then he thought of El Chango and the unloaded gun that cost him his life. Besides, it didn't solve the problem of having no place to go beyond the gate anyway. "It's heavy," Ned said, "but nice. Holding it, it feels natural."

The man chuckled. "Yeah, everyone compares the AK-47 to the American M-16. They say it is heavier, it is less accurate, not as powerful, it's not this, it's not that," he said. "But none of that matters. One grain of sand in your M-16 and it does not work; you are holding a toy gun. But you could put an AK-47 through the laundry, run over it with a truck, and throw it off a cliff and it would still work like it was brand-new. This is why we in the Third World like it. We freedom fighters. There's a reason why there are countries with AK-47s on the flag. It is a very effective weapon and it is cheap, especially the copies."

"Copies?"

"Oh yeah, there is such a demand for AK-47s that they are made all over the world," he said. "Some, like the Romanians or the Venezuelans, they will pay the Russians for the right to build them. Others, like the Chinese, the North Koreans, the Israelis, they just copy them. The Israelis are so smart. They sold the right to copy their copies to the Italians and South Africans."

"Is this a copy?" Ned said, handing the man back his gun.

"Nope, believe it or not, this is one of the real ones," he said proudly. "Made in the glorious Soviet Union."

"Soviet Union? Don't you mean Russia?" For a high-school dropout from the Midwest, Ned knew a surprising amount about the history and politics of Eastern Europe. After spending almost two years with the Russian mafia, and living with two different women from the region, he knew the differences between Romanians and Bulgarians and why the Croats still hate the Serbs after all these years.

"No, my new friend, the Soviet Union," the man said. "It was made in Mikhail Kalashnikov's own Izhmash factory in the city of Izhevsk in the Udmurt Republic of the Volga district of the Federation of Russia in the Union of Soviet Socialist Republics in 1981—like tens of millions of others."

"Really? It's that old?"

"But it works like a charm."

"Must be good workmanship."

"Nope, terrible workmanship, awful. Bad materials, too," the man said with a smile and a raised index finger. "But an excellent design."

Engaged in the conversation and sensing that this man had a story he wanted to tell, Ned threw caution to the wind. "How'd you get it?"

"That is a long story, one that may not interest you."

Ned made a show of looking around, then back at the man. "I have the time."

The man sighed, then smiled broadly. "Many years ago, when I was just a teenager, I received it from my father as he was being taken to prison. He told me in a code we had worked out between the two of us where I could find it.

He had hidden it in an old freezer in the basement of my uncle's restaurant."

"Why did he go to prison?"

"This is Mexico," the man said, as though speaking to a kindergartener. "He went to prison because somebody powerful did not like him. Anyway, you listen, don't interrupt, this is a good story. My old man was a rebel. Even though he was born into a wealthy family, he was outraged and disgusted by the injustices he saw all around him. The strong and greedy constantly preying on the poor and dispossessed. He hated the way Mexico was run, so he tried to stir up the peasants in the southern states to rebel against the wealthy whites—no offense intended, I'm all *Criollo* blood myself—who ran the country. It didn't take. Those dumb dirt famers wouldn't have understood Marx and Lenin if it was a puppet show. So he went to Cuba, but he didn't like it there either."

"Why not?"

"No faith in Castro and his brother. They had lost the revolutionary spirit; they had become exactly what they claimed they were fighting—wealthy autocrats who stamped out dissent by force," he continued. "When my old man saw Castro wearing an Adidas jogging suit, he flipped out. Not only was Adidas a huge multinational corporation that ran sweatshops all over the Third World, but it was founded by two Nazis and they even made sophisticated weapons for the Nazis to fight the powers of Bolshevism at the end of war."

"Really?"

The man sneered. "Yeah, Dad could not have been more pissed. So he went to Nicaragua where the Sandinistas were taking over. He really believed what they were selling—Ortega and those guys, land reforms, nationalization, right out of the old Soviet playbook."

"I vaguely remember something about that . . . Reagan, Bush, Oliver North . . ."

"Yeah, Reagan was actually right about what was going on, but he was stupid about how he handled it," the man continued with a sigh. "The Sandinistas were doing what the Soviets told them to do in exchange for weapons and cash. In fact, that's where my dad comes in. Ortega was building this secret airbase on the shores of Lake Nicaragua. It would have had the longest landing strip in all of Latin America, able to handle the Soviets' biggest transports, tankers, and bombers. At the same time, the Soviets were training Nicaraguan pilots to fly MiGs in Bulgaria. The Sandinistas thought they were in charge, but Dad knew it was all being run by some subcommittee back in Moscow."

"So your dad was a pilot?"

"Nope, he volunteered, but the Nicaraguans did not trust him because he was a Mexican *Criollo*, thought he might be a spy or at least not someone who could be trusted with too much responsibility," he said. "So they sent him to El Salvador to help with the civil war down there. Most everyone is white there, so they thought he'd fit right in."

"How did that go?"

"Not so good. Everyone likes the stereotype of the chubby, friendly Salvadoran, but they were not so much like that in the civil war—very violent, nasty business. Dad lost two fingers," he said with a serious look, holding down the two smallest fingers on his left hand to show Ned which ones his father was missing. "And it was a bad war; the rebels were in four separate groups that could never agree on anything—ideology, use of force, tactics, the role of women—so they never got anything accomplished. Then, when the Soviet Union fell apart, there was no more money, no more weapons; the rebels were forced to make peace with the government."

"And your dad?"

"He left long before that. I was born in 1984 and by then Dad had had enough with the Commies—realized they'd never win again and even when they did win, like Castro, they were no better than the guys they replaced. Look at the Chinese, a few assholes get rich running what is essentially a huge slave-labor camp and they have the nerve to call it Communism. Crazy!" He was getting angry now, his hands tightening around his rifle's stock and barrel. "So Dad comes back to Guadalajara and his parents want nothing to do with him. Why would a distinguished surgeon and an equally distinguished engineering professor have anything to do with a Commie rebel?"

Ned shrugged.

"So Dad went to work—funny, no? Communism is all about everyone working for the common good and this was the first time the old man had ever had a job in his whole life!" the man laughed. "He worked in a shoe factory."

"And he was arrested for being a rebel?"

"Aw, Espagueti, you let me down, I thought you were listening to me," the man smiled. "He was arrested because someone did not like him—maybe he was a better soccer player in school, maybe some girl liked him better, who knows?"

"Really? Is that how it works down here?"

The man turned pensive. "Yeah, that's why we are freedom fighters," he said. "For too long Mexico has been run by the hierarchy based on power and privilege. It's our duty to bring all that down."

Ned looked surprised. "So you guys are rebels. I thought you were drug traffickers."

The man looked very serious. "There is no reason why we can't be both."

Ned knew it was unwise to annoy a man with an AK-47 in his hand, so he changed the subject. "What are you doing up so early?" he asked. "Everyone else is asleep."

The man snorted in disapproval. "They all drink too much, smoke too much; not me," he said. "And you? Why are you up and around? Leaving so soon?"

Deflecting, Ned said that he couldn't sleep.

"Why not? There is lots of beer and plenty of weed."

"I don't drink or smoke much anymore," he said. It was technically true because since he had moved to Mexico he had very little money and even fewer friends. He knew he had free access to alcohol and drugs in the ranch house, but had decided to keep his wits about him, especially after what happened to El Chango.

"Coke, meth, you do those?"

"Never."

"Sounds like you've seen what they can do." The man smiled. "That's good, very smart," he said. "Go inside now, get one of the girls to cook you some food. You can eat it out back where it's nice. They will show you where." The man got up, took his gun, and walked about forty feet over to where a black Cadillac Escalade with tinted windows was parked. As he approached the car, the back-seat door opened from inside. The man first handed his gun to someone inside then got in the car itself. A moment later, it drove away. Ned was confused by what had just happened, but he knew he'd see the man again.

* * *

Even though Agent Tovar had assigned a junior agent and two interns to communicate with all the Indian parts suppliers in the United States and Canada, he had little hope any would actually cooperate with the agency. It was just another mountain of work that was dumped on him as Meloni and O'Malley pursued the more glamorous aspects of the case. The reason he had little faith in the dealers was because more than a few of them traded in parts under the table and even illegally to places like China and the United Arab Emirates where rich collectors would often pay a little extra to avoid mountains of paperwork.

But he persevered and he double-checked everything they found through established dealers, eBay, Craigslist, Kijiji, and other places people trade parts. He talked to the Indian owners' clubs and even a few motorcycle customizers he knew, but they adhered to the same code of silence as bikers because their business sometimes came from people who would rather not have their name bandied around. If word spread that a parts supplier or customizer was giving out information to law enforcement, their business would quickly become extinct.

Although he knew it would likely come to nothing, Tovar kept going on the Indian parts, not only because of the slim chance it could yield something but also because he often got his best, most creative ideas while concentrating on something else.

* * *

As instructed, Ned did ask one of the girls to make him something to eat and to show him the "nice place" out back. As soon as he said it, he thought she would take it as a euphemism for sex, and was relieved when she didn't. The girl, Juana, guided him to an area behind the house that was surrounded by trees (the trunks of which had been painted in the red, white, and green of the Mexican flag), flowers, and other decorative plants. The wall of vegetation not only sealed the little spot from the sun, making it about ten degrees cooler than the rest of the area, but it made a string of tiny white lights necessary. Combined with the pristine metal-and-glass furniture, the little glade had an idyllic appeal, nothing like the slovenly, drunken dorm-room atmosphere in and around the house.

Juana soon returned with a bowl of *puchero*, a thick beef stew laced with chickpeas, corn, squash, and other hardy vegetables that grew in the dry parts of northern Mexico. It had become a favorite of Ned's since he had moved to the area. He asked her to join him, to talk for a while. She sat, but seemed nervous, even jumpy. When she demurred about what her tasks were at the ranch and how she had gotten there, Ned let her return to her duties.

Ned thought about the women in the house. Most of the men he knew in Mexico were very strict about what they considered women's work, and never lifted a finger to help the women they knew, whether they were relatives or romantic partners. He also realized that the women were expected to provide the men of the house with sex any time they wanted it. Twice since he had been at the ranch house, women had offered him sex and he didn't think it was because of his looks or personality. It was clearly just part of the job.

His reverie was broken by a man calling him. It was El Guason. Ned emerged from behind the trees and approached him. "Hey, what's going on?" he asked.

"Time for work," he replied. "Same as yesterday, but this time, it's just me and you." El Guason led him through the ranch house, in which there were signs of life as men started waking up. One of them, Ned noticed, was wearing a police uniform. Once out of the house, El Guason and Ned walked over to a bright red Ford Mustang and got in. "My other car is a Corvette, but there's no room to carry anything," El Guason said to him. "All the other guys want trucks, they are a bunch of *güeys*, fresh off their dad's chicken ranch—they have no style." He pointed his thumb at the back seat of the car. It was filled with dozens of identical brown paper bags, each with the top folded over and stapled shut. Each one had a number written on it with a Sharpie.

As they drove down the dirt road, Ned noticed that they were again waved through the roadblock. Indeed, one of the cops politely moved his SUV so that El Guason could get through. "How are you finding everything—the house, the food? Good?" he asked Ned while waving at the cops without looking at them. "You're comfortable?"

Ned was surprised that El Guason would take such an interest in his welfare. "Yeah, I'm good," he said. "Just a little confused is all."

El Guason looked genuinely surprised. "Confused? Why?"

Ned didn't want to anger him, but couldn't help trying to get answers. "Well, I know I work for you now, but I don't know who you guys are."

El Guason snorted. "All you had to do was ask. We are just a group on entrepreneurs. The media calls us the Jalisco Cartel, but we prefer to be called the Rincon-Bravo Organization."

"Cartel?" Ned instinctively knew these guys were involved with a drug cartel, but hearing it from one of them still sent a jolt of panic though him.

El Guason laughed. "Don't let that word scare you; the DEA made it up to make us sound scary," he said. "Look, we know enough about you to know that dropping off bags of weed at gas stations, bars, and fruit stands isn't exactly the kind of work that will keep you awake at night."

Ned couldn't help but smile. "Yeah, I'll admit that I'm no stranger to this particular business," he said. "But when you say 'cartel,' it makes me think about a lot of money, a lot of violence." As they passed by the melon stand, Ned was reminded of El Chango's demise and it sobered him a great deal. He had been growing familiar with the ranch house, its people, and its way of life, but the image of the little Guatemalan being killed in front of him reminded him that he was being held captive and that he was still in an incredible amount of danger.

"There is money, no doubt, and some violence, too, but not the way you're imagining," El Guason told him as he threw his cigarette out the window and lit another. "But look at what you've seen—the cops are no problem here. People just buy our weed and pay us our money. We keep things quiet."

"Keep things quiet?"

"Yeah, this area used to be run by the Caro-Quintero Organization, what you people would call the Sonora Cartel, but when they went down, Sonora became a battleground between what you call the Tijuana Cartel and the Sinaloa Cartel. Bodies were everywhere—hanging from bridges, mailed in pieces to police stations, rotting in the streets." El Guason sounded bored as he described the carnage. "But there was a summit and it was decided that we would control this area—the TJs and the Sinaloans still get their cuts, but it's our place now."

"What do you mean by 'control'?"

El Guason looked at Ned like he thought he was stupid. "You know, sell weed, move product, pay off or threaten cops, keep the bad guys out," he said. "Just like you do up north."

"Seems like you're doing a great job."

"Yeah, every once in a while one of the old Caro-Quintero loyalists will do something stupid or a TJ will step on some toes," he said. "But they get taken care of pretty quickly."

El Guason wasn't trying to sound ominous, but that's how it hit Ned. He, too, was a member of a cartel. He wondered why they would want someone as conspicuous as him, with his blue eyes and halting Spanish, to be part of their group. But that was not the kind of question one asked El Guason.

Their first stop, just like their previous run, was a now-familiar Pemex station. El Guason parked outside and told Ned to take care of things. He went inside and was met by the one-handed cashier, Pedro. "Ivan is not here," he said. "You can just give me the bag."

Ned remembered that he had been told not to give the bag to Pedro. This could be a test, he thought to himself. And even if it wasn't, it could be the kind of classic fuck-up that could put him in a lot of trouble. "No, I can't," Ned told him. "I'll wait for Ivan."

"Could be a while." Pedro shrugged and went back to what he was reading. Ned had three choices: give the bag to Pedro, wait for Ivan (potentially angering El Guason who was idling in the Mustang outside), or go back to the car and ask El Guason what to do. Then he remembered something his boss at Hawkridge had told him—the best employee is one the boss doesn't have to worry about. He took that to mean that El Guason would have more respect for him if he solved the problem himself. He decided that he would wait for Ivan.

It did not take long. Ivan soon popped out of the door with the "Employees Only" sign while Ned was leafing through a stack of magazines, many of which were months out of date. "You're El Guason's *guero* friend," he smiled. "You have something for me?"

"Yes," Ned said, producing the bag. "And you have something for me?"

Pedro went behind the counter and pulled out a plastic bag full of cash. "It's all there," he said. "So, you're our man now?"

"Looks like," Ned said, nodding. "Can I get a bag of chips, those, the Barcels, the El Diablos, with lime."

Ivan handed him about a half-dozen bags. Ned said he only wanted one and asked how much they were. Ivan looked shocked. "For you? Nothing, everything in here is free for you. Here, take a couple of *pulques* with you, El Guason loves it." Ned couldn't stand the milky, opaque, and mildly alcoholic drink himself, but took both cans to shut the guy up and because he knew El Guason would indeed enjoy it.

Back in the Mustang, Ned handed the *pulque* to El Guason. "I was going to complain about how long you took, but not anymore," he said. "How did you know I love *pulque*?"

"Ivan told me," Ned said, handing him the bag with the cash.

El Guason took a swig of *pulque* and pointed to the back seat. "Just tie it up and throw it back there," he instructed. "That *pendejo* Pedro wasn't in there was he?"

"Yeah, he even asked me for the product," Ned told him.

"What? Really? That son of a whore," El Guason looked really angry.

"Why is it such a big deal?" Ned asked. "It's just a bag of weed, and it's not like we don't know where he works."

"You don't understand." El Guason, his voice rising. "Pedro can't handle anything. He's not allowed. He stole an entire kilo of meth from the Caro-Quinteros two years ago. Didn't you see his left hand had been cut off? He's a thief."

Of course Ned had noticed that Pedro was missing his left hand, but he hadn't read the significance of it. He had seen plenty worse since he'd arrived in Mexico. "Well, he didn't really ask for the bag, he just . . ."

"Don't try to defend him," El Guason said. Before Ned could reply, El Guason stopped at a car wash. Like most other cash washes in Sonora, this one—the Crystal Clear— was really just a couple of covered parking spots and some guys with hoses. "Okay, now take this package to Miguel Ricardo, not Miguel, Miguel Ricardo, you got that?"

Ned assured him he did and took the bag to the car wash's office. He asked for Miguel Ricardo and was directed to one of the guys sitting out front waiting for a car to wash. After making sure he was the right guy, Ned handed him the bag. Miguel Ricardo went into the office and returned with a thick manila envelope that he handed to Ned.

The pair continued to visit locations all over the south side of Nogales until all twenty-six bags of weed in the back seat had been replaced by twenty-six bags or envelopes of cash. This was going to be Ned's delivery route, said El Guason. He would take him around for the first week or so to get him familiar with the people and all the stops. After that, he said, Ned would do the route alone or with a friend if he had one he trusted. The organization would get him a car, find him a nice place to live, all he had to do was make deliveries. He would get 5 percent of the money he brought in. Ned asked if he would need to bring any muscle along, and El Guason laughed. "Nobody ever holds out," he said. "Nobody doesn't pay."

Ned knew it wasn't an ideal situation, but also that he didn't have much of a choice. It certainly beat the screen-door factory and it could be a springboard back to a little cash and independence. He agreed.

Ned slept at the ranch house that night and went with El Guason on the same route at about noon the next day. The first stop was the Pemex station. Ivan ran out to see Ned. Pedro wasn't there.

Ned never saw him again. But thousands did. During the night, someone hung Pedro's now completely handless body from a tree in the park on the east side of the city. Tied to it was a pair of signs—one in the front, one in the back. Both read "I stole."

Chapter Five

It was an absolutely beautiful morning. The sun hadn't scorched off all the moisture and coolness yet, so Ned sat on the veranda and looked at the ranch for the first time without assessing it for danger and possible escape strategies. Ordinarily, he was unimpressed by, even contemptuous of, Sonora's the dry, bleak landscape, but at this moment, it was ruggedly beautiful. His attention had turned to a little roadrunner that was frantically pacing among the scrub and occasional cactus on the lot in front of him, looking for lizards and snakes and caterpillars. Every time Ned moved, the roadrunner darted away, only to regain its confidence and scamper back.

Ned's five-day trial period with El Guason—the cartel worked Monday to Friday—was on its last day. It seemed to Ned to be going very well, but the two had not become friends. Ned found El Guason so obsessed by his appearance and possessions—especially his cars and jewelry—that they had little else to talk about. Of course, that didn't mean El Guason didn't talk. In fact, he went on and on, constantly bragging about this or that, as though he had a deep-seated need for Ned to be envious of him.

And, as Ned had experienced before when he joined the Sons of Satan, his immediate superior felt not just that he could tell Ned what to do all the time but also that Ned had to perform tasks and jobs that were well beneath him or even humiliating. Cleaning El Guason's guns and washing his cars were one thing, but doing his laundry and preparing his food was another. Ned noticed that none of the other men did such work, and wondered if his refusal to take advantage of the house girls—who came and went, sometimes on the same day—led them to believe he was less of a man than the rest of them.

It didn't matter now. If they were telling him the truth, it was the last day he'd have to ride with El Guason, who had told him that he was getting bored with teaching him the ropes and wanted to go back to his old job. When Ned asked what that job was, he quickly changed the subject.

The deal they had worked out was that, if Ned passed his trial period, the organization would set him up with a car and a place to live. Although Ned knew it was hardly an independent life, it would be a great step away from the claustrophobic feeling he had in the ranch house.

He was just killing time before one of the girls showed up. He had hoped Juana would be the first he'd see. He still hadn't managed to get three words out of her, but she was easily the best cook of the lot. If he could get her to whip him up something, he could retire to the nice spot out back and enjoy a few more quiet moments before the sun and work made life in Mexico a reality for him again.

As he walked back inside, he heard a phone ring. One of the men Ned knew simply as El Ardilla Voladora sprung awake from the sofa in the main room. He answered the phone, said yes a couple of times and hung up. Immediately, he started shouting for everyone in the house to get up. He ran upstairs and out back. Once the other men started to wake up, they all looked very serious. Every man in the house was doing something, obviously in preparation for a major event, but Ned didn't know what it was. When El Guason—who, as he often did, had stayed the night to avoid his sharp-tongued wife—appeared, Ned asked him what was going on.

El Guason looked startled, as though hearing Ned's voice had broken his concentration. "Oh, yeah, yeah, El Espagueti," he said. "This is not for you; go wait upstairs until I call you. I can send up . . . uh, uh . . . Monica." He paused as though he had caught himself in a faux pas. "To bring you some food."

"No, really, if it's part of my job . . ."

El Guason looked very angry. "Look, I've been told this is definitely not part of your job," he ordered. "Now, go upstairs, close the door, and stay in there until I or someone else comes to get you."

Ned knew better than to argue. Just as he was turning to go upstairs, he saw the front door burst open. Two Federales burst in with AR-15 assault rifles. Sure the shit was going down, Ned put his hands up. The first Federale laughed. "Put your hands down, you *guero* asshole," he said. "You're on our side."

Behind the two cops (who Ned quickly realized were members of his own organization in stolen uniforms) were three men who were in handcuffs. They were shirtless and masked. The first two shuffled silently behind the fake cops, while the third, a much smaller and younger man, wept and begged for his life. Behind them were six more armed men, one in a Sonora state police uniform, the rest in street clothes.

El Guason grabbed Ned by the arm. "Upstairs! Now!" he ordered. Ned complied, going directly to the room in which he slept. He immediately went to the window, but it pointed east and the group had gone out the back of the building on the south. Ned jumped when he heard the door open behind him. It was Monica, one of the girls. She sat on the bed, holding herself tight. She looked at Ned expectantly, then turned and looked straight ahead, rocking slightly on the edge of his bed. As Ned turned back to the window, two more girls rushed into his room—one he had never seen before and one whose name he could not remember—and joined Monica. They huddled together as though they were very, very cold.

Although he still couldn't see, Ned heard some indistinguishable shouting and then what sounded like popcorn popping, just a few random cracks that increased in frequency then died down. One of the girls screamed and began to cry. The others tried to calm her down, but were obviously stressed themselves. When the popping stopped, there was a quick *budda-budda*, sounding almost like a muffled drum roll, then a great deal of celebratory shouting.

Once the shouting started, the girl who had been crying fled from the room, running downstairs. The others followed her. Not knowing exactly what to do, Ned went downstairs, too. The men, led by El Ratón, were coming back in the house. They were smiling and laughing. El Guason ordered the girls to get them food and beer and to put on some music. They complied. As she was headed toward the kitchen, Monica was intercepted by one of the younger men. He grabbed her right hand and put his left around her waist, forcing her into a poorly executed waltz before releasing her to her duties. Clearly the men were celebrating.

Ned separated El Guason from the crowd. "What's going on?" he asked.

"Nothing, *guero*," he answered grinning. "It's a great day for the organization today, really good." He grabbed one of the younger men and held him firmly in a half-hug. "We have such good men, the best!" he boasted. "You know what? *Guero*, today is such a good day that you can do the route by yourself."

Ned wasn't sure why that announcement constituted a reward. But he knew it would be prudent to let El Guason stay and drink himself silly with the boys, so he agreed with what he hoped looked like enthusiasm. "I'll need a car," he said.

"Yeah, we got you one," El Guason said, and reached in his pocket for some keys, and handed them to Ned.

They were attached to a keychain with a figurine of a popular Mexican children's TV clown, Poco Loco. "I won't need this," he said, starting to remove the keychain. All the men within hearing distance laughed.

"Yes you will," El Guason told him sharply. "You get stopped by the cops or the army, just show them Poco Loco and tell them that's who you work for."

"Seriously?" Ned asked. "Poco Loco? The kiddies' clown?"

"Yeah, didn't you see mine?" El Guason held up his keys with a similar, but more battered keychain.

Ned told him that he hadn't, and the others laughed again.

"Just take the damn thing, and if you get into any trouble, the clown will get you out," his boss ordered. "The car's outside. It's a Mazda or some other thing I wouldn't be seen in. You can take the bags out of the back of the Mustang. It's unlocked."

*　*　*

Although she didn't like the Midwest as a rule, Agent O'Malley liked the time away from the office and its boys' club atmosphere. And it was also a chance to advance the case, which had shown little forward movement thus far. A suspicious fire at a warehouse in Hillsboro, Illinois, had attracted the agency's attention. Not only was the formerly sleepy town said to be a major distribution center for drugs, generally handled by bikers, but also the fire had all the hallmarks of an attempt to hide evidence. The crime scene investigators found a number of indications of fire accelerant (probably gasoline) and many items that one would rarely find in an abandoned warehouse. Among the suspicious items was the frame of an American-made motorcycle that was at least fifty years old. Meloni thought it could be the Indian that the FBI could link back to Ned Aiken. Bikes like that are rare. Aiken was originally from the Midwest and the fact that organized crime was probably involved also pointed to him.

She had privately hoped that all the local cops wouldn't be shaven-headed muscle boys or beer-bellied goofballs, but she was disappointed. The evidence had long been removed from the scene, and she was taken to the Montgomery County sheriff's department to see the frame. She'd been e-mailed some details, but they weren't very specific. The locals had determined it was American made, somewhere between 1946 and 1953. It was probably an Indian, but could have been any of a number of different makes.

It didn't look like much to O'Malley, just a piece of twisted metal with burn marks and ash stuck to it. The Montgomery cops had brought in a local expert. He was a short man, but not small. Maybe five-foot-three, he must have carried over 300 pounds on him. Despite it being indoors, he wore a broad-brimmed straw hat. Long strands of white hair stuck out from underneath it, in contrast to his much darker beard. He took off his hat to shake the agent's hand, revealing a bald head and a wide, red face with thick-lensed, wire-framed glasses.

"Ma'am, am I to understand that the motorcycle frame you are seeking is that from a 1948 Indian?" he asked in a condescending tone.

"Yes," O'Malley said, looking at her notes. "It's a 1948 . . ."

"I don't need to know the model, ma'am," he interrupted her, holding up his hands to shush her. "This is a 1951 or later . . . I can tell because of the welding style. It's not your frame."

O'Malley smiled. She was used to such treatment. "Your opinion will be noted in the record," she said as officiously as she could. "But it is now the property of the FBI. I'll have my people ship it to FBI headquarters Quantico; if it's not the one we want, we will send it back for your local investigation." She did not wait for any arguments. Instead, she beckoned to the team of agents she'd brought to remove the frame, then turned on her heel and walked out to her rental car.

* * *

Ned left the celebration behind and walked out to the barren area where the men parked their cars. Immediately and without question, he could tell which car was his. Nestled in among the brightly colored and gaudily customized pickups and SUVs was one small, plain-looking sedan. It wasn't a Mazda as El Guason had guessed, but rather an ancient and battered Subaru Impreza. The reliability and sensibility of small, Japanese cars had yet to win over any of the Mexican men he knew, most of whom considered a truck of some sort to be absolutely vital to one's masculinity.

The Subaru was a sand color on the outside, and inside it was decorated with religious symbols and a few photos and stickers of kittens. It smelled vaguely of what Ned guessed was lavender. As he packed the back-seat full of the now familiar paper bags full of weed, Ned sighed behind the wheel and thought about the car's former owner. The way the interior had been treated indicated that it was a young woman. The make, model, and age indicated she was not wealthy, but at least had a steady income. He hoped that the loss of her car hadn't endangered that.

Ned realized it was pointless to worry about someone else when he considered the position he himself was in and gave a little chuckle as he turned the key. As soon as he passed the two guys at the gate, who waved at him, he realized he could be free. He had a little car, a tank full of gas, about three dozen bags of weed, and a gun (which, he made sure, was full of ammo). He could collect the cash for the weed and make a dash for it. "But where would you go, idiot?" he said to himself. Escaping these guys was still his eventual plan, but it was ridiculous to do anything about it now. These dudes would kill you for a dollar, let alone thousands. Sure he was armed, but what was a mere popgun when they had dozens of AK-47s? Besides, even though he had once accidentally killed a guy, he wasn't exactly the kind of person who'd be able to shoot his way to freedom. He'd need more money, he'd need contacts and, most of all, he'd need a place to go.

Ned was driving the familiar route into town when he slowed down for the roadblock. He had never seen any of the Federales there before, and noticed that one was pointing an assault rifle at him as he stopped and rolled down the little car's window. Experience had taught him to look at the type of gun any cop in Mexico was carrying as a first step in determining whether he was legitimate or not. This guy had an AR-15, which could go either way. Although the

Federales did issue them, they were also very popular with the cartels. At least these guys were clean shaven, although some had conspicuous gold on their persons.

Another cop came up to the window and asked for Ned's driver's license. He produced the one his old boss, El Orangután, had made for him. When they asked for registration, he made a move for the glove box (even though he had no idea what was inside) when the guy with the assault rifle nervously shouted: "Keep your hands where I can see them! Keep your hands where I can see them!"

Ned complied and the other cop asked him to step out of the car. "I don't like the look of this at all," said the cop. He was a very short man, who seemed not to be a very quick thinker as he meticulously pored over the driver's license and into the car. "Mr. Duncan, this picture on your license, it does not look like you."

In fact, the picture *was* of him. It was the only honest part of the whole situation. This was one of those moments that happen frequently in Mexico and other parts of the world, but are still hard for most North Americans to judge. Ned was not sure if the cops were seriously going to investigate him or just wanted a bribe. The little cop with his license refused to look him in the eye, which made Ned think it would be just a matter of a few hundred pesos, but the guy with the AR-15 was definitely serious. His nervousness and his finger on the trigger unsettled Ned a great deal. Finally, the little man handed Ned his license back. "We could take care of this downtown, or . . ." He left the sentence hanging.

Relieved that these guys just wanted a few bucks, Ned nodded, and said, "If I could just pay the fine here . . ."

He started to reach into his pocket when he realized he didn't have any money. "Oh, it seems that I have forgotten my money at home," he said. "Would you mind if I just . . ." Before he could finish, a third cop knocked him to the ground. The barrel of the assault rifle was now pressed against the back of his head.

"Arrest him," ordered the little cop angrily. The third cop stood Ned up, frisked him, and put him in cuffs. A fourth went into the car, shouting back that the back seat was full of weed. Then he shut off the idling Subaru and handed his boss the keys.

"Holy shit!" the little man said with a mixture of surprise and terror. "How did you get this?" He ran up to Ned with the keychain. "Tell me why you have this?"

Ned remembered that El Guason had told him to show the little clown to anyone who bothered or threatened him. "My boss gave that to me, told me to carry it wherever I go."

"Who's your boss?" asked the third cop.

"Shut up!" shouted the little cop. "Don't ask him any more questions! Pablo, apologize for hitting Mr. Duncan! Take the cuffs off!"

Pablo did as he was told. The little cop returned Ned's belongings to him and said, "I'm very sorry for this little inconvenience. Please don't think it will ever happen again." He sounded absolutely frantic. The guy with the assault rifle started yelling something. "Put the gun down, you idiot!" shouted his boss. "Can't you see our new friend here is a very important man?"

Ned, suddenly aware that these men were very afraid of him and pissed off that they had treated him so very roughly, decided to press his luck. "Thank you, gentlemen," he said. "As you recall, I mentioned that I left my cash at home. Could I trouble you to loan me a few pesos until Friday?"

A look of shock and terror came over the three men. After a quick whip-round, they produced just over 300 pesos and the little one, the one in charge, handed it over to Ned.

He climbed back into the Subaru and waved good-bye.

* * *

There was a knock on Agent Meloni's door. It was Dudley Weise, the intern. Weise was a big man, who had tried out for a couple of NFL teams before accepting an internship from the agency. He'd graduated magna cum laude in criminology from a small school in Mississippi, and he was constantly correcting people's pronunciation of his last name, which was "Wise," not "Weeze." Tovar liked him, Meloni knew. Unlike the more jaded agents he worked with, Weise often provided a different perspective, a fresh way of looking at things. He had a knack for finding details other officers would not see because they were looking for more specific clues.

"I have something here," he said. "Something on this Ned Aiken guy."

"Really?" Meloni was intrigued. So little of consequence had happened on that front, he was grateful for any news.

"Yeah, remember the girl said they stopped to buy some helmets?" he said. "I think I found out where."

"I thought we checked all the biker places."

"We did, but from the girl's description of the dealership and of the helmets, it made me think it wasn't a Harley shop." Weise said. "Then I remembered this guy is a former biker on the run. The last people he wants to see—besides us, that is—would be more bikers. So I looked at all the places where you can buy helmets and that are not associated with bikers on what I have figured to be their route."

"Interesting theory."

"It gets better," Weise paused for effect. "I've found a Suzuki dealer in Edgemoor, who said he sold two helmets to a man off the street who just happened to have a young girl with him, a young girl who seemed not to speak any English—and the date, time, and descriptions all match." Weise was grinning perhaps too proudly for Meloni's liking, but he was impressed at the kid's ability to see beyond the obvious line of inquiry.

"Good work," he told him. "I'm sending Tovar. I don't often send interns with them, but this was your thing, so why don't you tag along?"

* * *

Nobody talked. When Ned made his rounds that day, he was surprised by the fact that the people who were his contacts, the people he dropped the bags to and who paid him, wanted nothing to do with him. They wouldn't say "hello" or "good-bye" and really tried not to look at him. In the factory, he found Mexicans—the men at least—to be friendly and outgoing, though perhaps a little bit cagey. But these people treated him like he was a ghost. They were polite, even respectful, to be sure, but offered as little of themselves—even eye contact—as was possible.

That changed about two-thirds of the way through his route. At another Pemex station, the connection was a fat man with an elaborate cowboy hat. Although he didn't look directly at Ned, he did tell him to meet him back at the station after he was finished his run. Figuring it was another test, Ned agreed.

The rest of his route went easily, as he was now familiar with all the stops and somewhat less unnerved by the cold shoulder the connections were giving him. His run-in with the cops made him understand that the Jalisco Cartel was a group much respected, or at least feared, and as their representative, he too was to be feared. That also led him to understand that all he had to do was walk into a bar with a bag of weed and get paid in full without any argument. It was never that way north of the border where retailers were always crying poor, shorting their stacks, or trying one way or another to get out of paying. He actually kind of liked the idea of this job. In about ninety minutes, he pulled in enough so that his cut was a couple hundred dollars' worth of cash every day he worked. By Mexican standards, that was pretty good money. He could put away some and . . . and that's where the thought ended. He didn't know where to go in the long term. But right now, he knew, he had to go back to the Pemex station.

The fat man in the cowboy hat shook his hand and told him his name was Rodrigo. "Your boss, he called me," he told Ned without looking at him. "I have something for you, to give to you."

Ned was surprised. Rodrigo had already paid for his shipment. Perhaps he was behind and had to make up for an old debt, but why couldn't he have taken care of that on

Ned's first visit? He certainly looked depressed about this whole business. "What is it?" Ned asked.

Rodrigo sighed and still refused to look up. "He says I have to show you," he said. "If you drive me, I will give you directions."

A cold shot ran through Ned. He'd seen something similar to this before. The bikers he knew would offer to drive someone somewhere for a surprise—maybe a party, maybe even a patch—and the guy would never get there. Although the men he was working for had no reason to kill him, Rodrigo could be working for anyone. He could be from a rival gang, could just be pissed off, or this could even be a robbery attempt—everyone knew the Subaru was full of cash after a run. And Ned did not think it paranoid that he let his mind wander enough to think this guy could be hired by bikers or even the FBI. The fact that he would not look at him made him a lot less trustworthy. "No thanks," Ned told him, and began to back out of the store.

Rodrigo looked stunned. "But you have to . . ." he pleaded, "or my son . . ."

"What? What about your son?"

"Nothing, nothing, it's just I have orders I have to follow, just like you," Rodrigo said beseechingly. "And your boss was very, very clear that you must receive this . . . gift."

Ned thought for a moment. He knew El Guason was not his boss, and that he was being tested. This could be a trap, he thought, but he was in danger no matter what he did, so he opted to believe the obviously desperate man. "Do you have a gun?" he asked.

"Yes, under the counter."

"Step away from the counter," Ned said, and moved behind the counter once Rodrigo was clear of it. Although the chance of an ambush still existed, at least he wanted Rodrigo unarmed. He saw an old cigar box, opened it, and took out a cheap-looking handgun. He took out the magazine and emptied the chamber. "Got any more weapons?"

Rodrigo sighed. "A knife in my boot."

"What side?"

"Right."

"Your right or my right?"

"Mine."

"Take it out."

Even though Ned had not drawn his gun, Rodrigo complied nervously, pulling the knife out of his boot and sliding it across the floor to Ned. A customer walked into the store, sensed the tension, turned around and walked back out.

"Okay," Ned said. "You drive. I'll be in the back seat."

Rodrigo closed the store and took the keys from Ned. "Poco Loco," he said as he noticed Ned's key ring. "I used to watch him when I was a kid. Sad what happened though."

"What happened?"

"His daughter, you know?"

"No I don't know," Ned said. When Rodrigo opened the front door, Ned remembered the bags of cash in the back seat. "Can you move that stuff to the trunk?"

Rodrigo agreed and started to collect the money, inserting loose cash into various bags while taking them to the trunk. "I guess you weren't in Mexico then. It was huge news," he said. "His daughter, Kelli, a really beautiful young girl, became a pop singer."

"That sounds like a good thing."

"It was, until she sang the wrong song," he said. "At a concert in Juarez, she sang *To All My Enemies*, which is the theme song of the Sinaloa Cartel. That really pissed off the Gulf Cartel."

"Yeah, and?"

Rodrigo looked him in the eye. "They kidnapped her from her hotel—in front of dozens of witnesses—held her prisoner for two weeks in which she was raped by dozens of men," he said. "Then all of her body except her head was delivered to her father's studio one piece at a time."

"That's awful," Ned said. "What happened to the old man?"

Rodrigo laughed mirthlessly. "He kept the show going, but it was depressing," he said. "Instead of fun and entertainment, it was all focused on keeping children safe . . . it was awful . . . then he finally shot himself in the head."

Ned, dumbfounded, realized they were just standing there and directed Rodrigo to get in the front of the car, while he got in the back. Although he was beginning to believe Rodrigo meant him no harm, he drew his gun anyway, and slipped off the safety. "Okay, let's go," Ned said. After Rodrigo started the car, he asked: "What ever happened to the head?"

Rodrigo chuckled. "I never thought about it until now," he said. "I guess they gave it a decent burial."

* * *

The Suzuki dealership in Edgemoor was bright, tidy, and welcoming. Like many retailers of Japanese bikes, it had a dual personality. One-half of the showroom was dedicated to sport bikes and it was decorated with wild colors and graphics. The other side, devoted to cruisers—what companies that are not Harley-Davidson call Harley-Davidson-style bikes—was dark and malevolent. A young, well-muscled, and tattooed guy in shorts and a Suzuki golf shirt greeted Weise and Agent Tovar and introduced himself as Sam, the manager. He then directed them to George Tassiopoulos, the clerk who had served the two people in question.

He looked about nineteen, and Sam explained that George was working at the dealership to pay for college. After introducing them, Sam took the officers and the witness into an office they normally used to close deals and explain financing options. George seemed more excited than nervous. Tovar, the experienced agent, started with the questions. "Just tell me about these two people you saw," he said.

"Well, at first I didn't think much of them," George said. "Just a guy and his daughter or something. But then I noticed he was sweaty and nervous, and they didn't talk even though he was putting helmets on her to get the right fit."

"Really?" said Weise, looking at Tovar. "Go on."

"Yeah, when I went to help them, he was kind of rude," he said. "And it was clear the little girl couldn't speak English—and it was almost like he couldn't understand her language either."

"So what was she speaking?" asked Tovar. "Spanish?"

"No, no, I know lots of Spanish from school and the kids I play baseball with," George told them. "This was like Russian or something."

Weise shot Tovar a look. "Really?"

"Yeah, I speak a little Greek and it definitely wasn't Greek, but it might have been from around there," he said. "She was dressed strange, too—not like the girls around here, like a younger kid . . . cheap, silly-looking clothes."

Tovar showed George photos of both subjects—Sopho from the day she was discovered by police, Ned from when he entered witness protection. "Oh, yeah, that's definitely her—even wearing the same clothes," George said. "He's a bit harder to tell; looks like him, but I can't be 100 percent sure."

"Did you notice anything strange about them?" asked Weise.

"What wasn't strange about them?" George answered. "Guy comes in here, looking desperate and sweaty. He has a girl with him, might actually be a little too old to be his daughter now that I think of it, and probably too young to be his sister. And she doesn't speak a word of English. He tells me he wants two full-face helmets—made it clear they had to cover their faces entirely—won't talk about what kind of bike he has or where he's from. And he paid in cash—had a roll of twenties and hunnies big as my fist."

Tovar laughed. "Did he say anything? Anything at all about where he was going or what he was doing?"

George thought back. "Not really," he said. "Wait, there was one thing. He bought the girl a jacket. A leather jacket.

I convinced him that if he was taking the girl on a bike she'd need one."

"Commission sales?" Tovar asked.

"Nope, hourly," George said. "But what's good for the store is good for me. It was this one here." He pointed at a blue-and-yellow jacket with a big "S" for Suzuki on the back in a catalog. Tovar took a copy of the catalog with him and gave George his business card in return, telling him to call him if he remembered anything else.

* * *

As they drove together through the south side of Nogales, Ned didn't exactly come to trust Rodrigo, but he did lose much of his fear of him. Rodrigo opened up to him, told him about his family, his life. His was an old Sonora family, "real cowboys." His ancestors had never owned any land or cattle, but were experts at herding them on the long trails from the ranches to the slaughterhouses, often hundreds of miles away. Of course, the national highway system and semi-trailers changed all that. "There is no art or beauty left to the production of beef anymore," he complained. "Now they lock a cow in a closet, force it to eat shit, and when it's fat enough, they drag it to the truck and then drag it to slaughter. Not like the old days when it was man against beast."

With no cowboy work to do, his father had a hard time finding work. When he died in a slaughterhouse accident, Rodrigo had to quit school and go to work. He had been working for Pemex ever since and had been padding his pay packet however he could. "I don't want you to think

Mexicans are bad people," he said to Ned. "These are just bad times."

"What were the good times like?"

"I can't remember any."

They pulled into a quiet neighborhood surrounded on three sides by high rocky hills. It was called Las Bellotas even though Ned had not seen an oak tree anywhere near the place. It was like any North American grid-plan subdivision, except the narrow houses were all made of the same color of poured concrete and every door and window had metal bars on it. Some of the houses had been painted, and Rodrigo pulled into the driveway of a yellow one on Calle Higueras. It was two doors down from a house that had been converted to a grocery store.

Out front there was a woman and three kids—a boy of about eleven, a girl of nine, and a smaller boy she was holding. Each of the older children had a shopping cart full of possessions and the woman had more items in a baby stroller. They stared at Rodrigo and Ned as they left the car. Ned hid his gun from the kids' view. He instructed Rodrigo to go in the house and come back out while he waited in the driver's seat. Rodrigo did as he was told. "Can I give you your gift now, Mr. Suspicious?" He smiled.

"I guess you can."

Rodrigo handed him some keys. "The house, it is yours," he said. "Yours to use, to live in. Your boss still owns it, though."

Ned was surprised. He knew they'd get him a place to live, but thought it would be an apartment somewhere, maybe with some other guys, not what looked like a three-bedroom house. Inside, it was furnished with tables and chairs, beds, and sofas. All the big items of family life were there, but nothing small, the things you'd need for daily life, like clothes, blankets, or cooking utensils. Ned told himself he could get them later. He explored the house and decided he liked it far better than staying at the ranch house or even in the apartment Holsamex had set up for him.

In fact, it was quite nice. It even had a tiny backyard with some cactuses and a small fig tree. It was made very private with a high concrete fence and Ned could see himself eating breakfast out there. Satisfied this was where he wanted to live, he offered to give Rodrigo a ride back to the Pemex station. He agreed and they shook hands. Rodrigo had a warm smile on his face.

As they walked outside. The eleven-year-old boy shouted at Rodrigo. "Hey! *Pendejo!* Why are you taking our house?"

Rodrigo snarled at the boy and made a gesture that indicated he'd smack him with the back of his hand if he came any closer. "Ask your father!" he shouted back.

The boy, his eyes wild, then looked directly at Ned, spat on the ground, and ran his index finger across his throat.

There were a lot of things Ned needed to get used to in Mexico, but he never thought being afraid of children would be one of them.

Chapter Six

The kid had freaked Ned out, but it didn't take long to shake it off. Rodrigo had asked to go home instead of back to the Pemex station. His wife said that she couldn't let Ned go back to an empty house, so she gave him some old pots, pans, silverware, blankets, and towels to bring back to his new home. She wouldn't accept anything in return, so Ned slipped each of their children a 100-peso note.

Since the money from the collections was in the trunk, Ned put the gifts from Rodrigo's wife in the back seat and drove back to the ranch house. Once he dropped off the money, he was basically free for the weekend. He had a house, a car, a gun, and some cash. Things were looking up. He planned on heading to the mall and grabbing some things to make his new home a little nicer.

Once he arrived at the ranch house, he handed the money off to El Guason, who was drunk, and thanked him. El Guason asked him why he thanked him. "The house, man," Ned said. "It's great."

"What house?"

"The new house, the house I live in now," Ned said with one eyebrow cocked. "Rodrigo told me you gave it to me."

"I didn't give anyone anything; I don't give anyone anything," he answered, looking confused. "Are you sure he said me? Did he say El Guason or Antonio López Ortega?"

"Neither, he said my 'boss.'"

El Guason laughed. "I'm not your boss, you stupid *guero*!" he cackled. "I'm just your teacher." Then he put a more serious look on his face. "Wait, he gave you a fucking house?"

Ned was no closer to learning who "he" was, but he could tell El Guason was drunk and angry and it would not be a good idea to start asking questions. "Just a little place to stay," Ned said. "Not too far from here."

El Guason appeared to calm down. "I knew he had some plans for you, but that's pretty good," he smiled. "Still driving that piece-of-shit car, though?"

Ned laughed in what he hoped would be taken in a self-deprecating way. "Yeah," he said. "It beats walking."

El Guason agreed and told Ned he'd have to have a party soon, invite everyone. He wasn't going to be around anymore, but someone would be able to reach him. Ned knew that El Guason was looking forward to going back to his regular job, but he didn't know exactly what it was or when he was leaving. He wouldn't miss him.

"So who's my contact gonna be on Monday?" Ned asked.

El Guason smiled. "Oh shit, yeah, the weed," he said, as though he hadn't thought about it for a while. "Well, it was going to be Johnny Irlanda, but he's leaving the company. How about El Martillo, you like him?"

In fact, Ned didn't actually "like" too many of the guys he'd met at the ranch house, but he guessed that El Martillo, a guy who looked enough like El Guason that he thought they might be brothers, was tolerable enough. He certainly wasn't as stupid or quick to anger as most of the guys. "Yeah," he said. "That's fine. Are you gonna tell him?"

"Yeah, yeah, over the weekend."

That didn't inspire Ned's confidence. By now, he'd learned that El Guason came by his nickname ("the lazy one") honestly. "Maybe I'll have one of the girls tell him," he suggested.

"No!" shouted El Guason. "The girls know nothing."

"But they're always around and you guys talk about everything in front of them all the time." Ned was confused.

"The girls know nothing," he was calming down. "I will tell El Martillo when I see him. Until then, take your shitty car to your shitty house and start making plans for a big party."

Ned laughed, but only to please El Guason. He would miss neither him nor the ranch house. He ran upstairs to collect the few things he was storing under his bed, mostly clothes. It then occurred to him that he would not have to start from scratch again. All he had to do was head back to the old apartment he had lived in when he worked at Holsamex. The industrial district wasn't far from Las Bellotas anyway. The Subaru wasn't very big, but he could move all his stuff in a couple of trips.

Approaching from the south, the city more or less begins where the signs on Highway 15 start calling it the Álvaro Obregón. Ned was headed north when he noticed traffic was locked up just before the Luis Donaldo Colosio Murrieta overpass. Cars were stopped and didn't look like they were going to move again soon. There was no oncoming traffic and Ned actually thought about driving in those lanes to get around the jam, but he didn't want to draw too much attention to himself.

He noticed that people were getting out of their cars and walking, even running, toward the overpass. Curious, Ned put the car in park and turned off the engine. He pulled the keys out of the ignition and tucked them in his pants pocket, careful to keep the clown keychain well hidden. Then he took his gun out of the glove compartment and hid it in a paper bag, taking it with him to see what all the excitement was about. The crowd was murmuring, but it was too low for Ned to understand. None of the people would look him in the eye. The further he got into the crowd, the less noise they were making. When he could finally see what the commotion was about, he understood the solemnity.

A man's corpse hung from the overpass, spinning and twisting on yellow nylon rope. Ned's stomach spun in revulsion and horror. It was facing away from him, but he didn't need to see the face to know who it was. Dressed in the same kind of jeans, boots, and a bright shirt almost all Sonoran men wore, it could have been anybody. But Ned knew it was Johnny Irlanda, who had earned his nickname ("Johnny Irish") because, like El Orangután, his repeated attempts to dye his hair blonde had caused it to turn bright red. So this was what El Guason meant by "leaving the company."

Vibrations from a passing semi spun the body around. It was indeed Irlanda, but somebody had taken the time to paint clown makeup on his face. And there was a sign tied to his body. It was handwritten but very clear: "Poco Loco says: Don't Tattle!" Underneath was a crudely drawn smiley face.

* * *

Agent Meloni was impressed that Tovar and his intern Weise had managed to track down Sopho's jacket. He was more than intrigued by who ended up with it—Thor Andersson. According to them, the jacket and helmet had been found in a public garbage pail near the corner of 48th and 11th on Manhattan's West Side by Dave Lombard, an editor at a technology-related newspaper. He had given the jacket to his son, but sold the helmet online because he didn't want to encourage his son to ride a motorcycle. The boy liked the jacket, but found Andersson's business card in the pocket with a handwritten note on the back that read: "Please take me to Thor Andersson" and gave his business address.

The boy and his dad then went to see Andersson. They gave him the jacket—which he seemed surprised about, claiming never to have seen it before—and the dad offered him money for the helmet he had sold. Andersson took the jacket, but refused the cash, instead paying the boy a reward that the dad thought was a bit excessive, perhaps more than the jacket was even worth.

Lombard contacted police after an art director he worked with had shown him an article in a local tabloid that had pictures of the helmet and jacket and a telephone number to call. The story said that the items could be connected to some serious crimes. At the time, investigators called it a coincidence. "This Andersson guy's not some kind of criminal, is he?" he asked, concerned. "He seemed so . . . upstanding. Like a good guy."

"That's all I've ever heard about him, what a great guy he is," Meloni answered. "To tell you the truth, Mr. Lombard, I can't really discuss that sort of thing with you, but I *can* tell you that you are not in any trouble or danger."

"That's a relief," he said. "Can we keep the money?"

Meloni was unsure of what money he meant until he remembered the reward for finding the jacket. "That's not a problem."

* * *

It took Ned all night to get back to the new place. A couple of army trucks came in and cut Irlanda down and restored traffic. By the time things were moving again, Ned had eaten a full meal since street vendors, eager to take advantage of the huge crowd, moved in immediately.

After a while, as the food and no small amount of beer and *pulque* circulated and music played, people calmed down and waited. It was a convivial atmosphere. Not quite a party, but far from the somber atmosphere that had pervaded the mob when the body was first discovered. Ned milled around in the crowd. Nobody paid much attention to him. After a while, he spotted one of his weed contacts. Alex was a tall and skinny young man who drove a minibus. Since most of the workers at the factories are women, the companies often supply small vans with drivers to bring them to work and drop them home again safely. Alex also sold Ned's weed to the husbands, brothers, boyfriends, and sons of the women he ferried back and forth.

Ned approached him. Alex acknowledged him grudgingly. Ned asked if he was working. "Yeah, just two left," he said and motioned over to two middle-aged women sitting on a blanket drinking Diet Cokes. They did not look up. "But I don't have all your money yet."

Ned smiled. "That's okay, dude, I'm not collecting right now, just stuck in traffic: I'll get you tomorrow morning, as usual," he said. "What do you think of all this?"

Alex looked at him suspiciously. "It happens. I guess it's to show us not to do anything against the boss."

"The boss?"

Alex looked at him angrily. "Yeah, your boss," he said. "The clown."

"What? Poco Loco is my boss? The Poco Loco?" Ned said, confused. El Guason said that neither he nor El Martillo were his boss, just his teachers. Ned was flooding the area with weed, but had no idea where it came from. El Guason had said something about the Jalisco Cartel, but that meant nothing to Ned. Obviously, the clown figure was some kind of symbol to these men, but how could he be anything more? Up until then, he had thought the Poco Loco thing was a gag, or perhaps someone's nickname, but now with all the strangeness of Mexico unfolding in front of him, he couldn't tell what was real and what wasn't.

"Poco Loco? Isn't he dead?"

Alex looked aghast. "Not so loud! You'll be a dead clown, like your friend up there," he grabbed Ned by the arm and led him to a more secluded area. "The very last thing I want to do is piss off a man in your position, but I think you really should know more about exactly who you are working for." Alex then separated from Ned and said, "With all due respect to you and the organization, I really don't think it's a very good idea for us to be seen together right now." Then he turned and walked toward the two women on the blanket.

* * *

Back in Andersson's office, Meloni told him he just had to ask a few questions that had come up relating to the Ned Aiken/Eric Steadman case. Andersson said he would do everything in his power to help.

"Great, do you remember receiving a blue-and-yellow leather jacket with a Suzuki logo on the back?" Meloni asked. "It was brought to you here at the office."

Andersson looked genuinely surprised. "Yes, yes I do remember that jacket," he said. "A man and his son brought it in all the way from New York City. I had never seen it before, but they said that it had my name inside, so I accepted it and thanked them."

Meloni nodded. "Actually, it was more than that, they said; it actually had your business card in a pocket," he said. "And a handwritten note that said 'Bring me to Thor Andersson.'"

"Really? I didn't get that detailed in my discussion with them," he answered. "I was very busy and considered the jacket almost a trivial matter."

"Don't you find that odd?" Meloni pressed. "I mean, here we have a leather jacket you have never seen before, one specifically designed for protection for motorcycle riders—a jacket made for a child but that has your name in the pocket?"

"Yes, yes I do," Andersson said, seemingly without worry. "I thought it was strange at the time, too."

"And the fact that it said 'me' and not 'this' bothers me a little," Meloni told him. "I mean, who calls their jacket 'me'?"

"There are lots of people with poor language skills out there," Andersson grinned. "And several of them work for me."

Meloni chuckled. "It is definitely true that few people pay enough attention to grammar," he said. "But it just makes me think." Realizing Andersson would reveal no more about the note, he turned to the jacket itself and he changed tones from jovial to inquisitive. "So why did you even take the jacket? I mean, the little boy really seemed to like it."

Andersson laughed. "Yes, yes he did," he agreed. "But my feeling was if it was brought to me, it must have been for one of my employees who thought the office was a safe place to deliver it." Then he smiled. "And to tell you the absolute truth, it looked a little bit . . . uh . . . girly on him, you know, too feminine—I was saving him from himself," he said. "And if someone wanted me to hold onto the jacket for them, who am I to argue?"

"But who would want you to have a jacket like that?"

"I have no idea," Andersson told him. "I held onto it for thirty days, put a sign up in the lunchroom, but nobody claimed it."

"I see." Meloni paused, hoping to make Andersson uncomfortable, but it didn't seem to work. "If you remember anything else about the jacket, please give me a call."

Andersson said he would.

"He won't call," Meloni thought to himself, "but I will come back when I have something more concrete."

* * *

While getting ready for a much-needed day off from delivering weed, Ned was surprised to hear the buzzer for his intercom as he stepped out of the shower. Whoever wanted to talk to him was persistent and did not seem likely to go away. Ned wrapped a towel around his waist, grabbed his gun, and looked at the intercom's tiny monitor. It was one man, alone. He was almost bouncing with nervous frustration. He had the same kind of Guatemalan or Mayan look as the unfortunate El Chango, but was dressed in the collared shirt, boots, and jeans that all men over a certain age in Sonora seemed to wear. He had a baseball cap on that made him look younger than his thirty-five or so years.

Ned answered, trying to sound tough. "What do you want?" he asked in Spanish.

"I have been sent to pick up El Espagueti," the little man said in a thick accent. "He has work to do."

"Who sent you?"

"I don't know the guy's name," the little man said angrily. "One of the Jalisco guys . . . tall, ugly, bad skin . . . I forget his name. You know, the guy who spits when he talks."

Ned laughed a little. "And who are you?" It was beginning to occur to him that none of the parties who'd like to get their hands on him would be stupid (or cunning) enough to send this guy to his front door. No, depending on who it was, he'd either be surrounded by an army of cops or someone would bomb the house or an assassin would sneak in. It just would not happen this way.

The man on the intercom sighed. "They call me El Chango."

Was this a joke? He knew a lot of Mexicans were religious and superstitious, but did this mean they thought he—an American—believed in ghosts? Maybe it was a warning: "Do what they say or end up like El Chango." As the initial shock wore off, Ned realized it was just more likely that northern Mexicans call all indigenous Mexicans, or at least the Guatemalan ones, *chango* just like they called any non-Hispanic whites *guero* whether or not they were blonde.

Before Ned had collected his thoughts enough to formulate an appropriate answer, the little man spoke again. "He gave me a note to read to you—it's in English even," he said. Ned could see him reach into his pocket and pull out a piece of crumpled-up paper. The new El Chango read from it intently. "Gate chore hass to ta ranjowsessho . . . esshowl." He returned to Spanish. "Some of these words, they are very hard, I am not even totally fluent in Spanish, but English is like it came from the moon for me."

Ned laughed and hit the lock release on the wrought-iron gate. "Come in, El Chango," he said. "I just stepped out of the shower and need to get dressed."

"I would actually prefer to stay here if it is okay with you, sir."

"Suit yourself," Ned said, then turned to put his clothes on. He packed his gun, his cell phones, and a little bit of cash, and went outside. The new El Chango smiled. Ned was surprised to see that the man's head did not come up to his own chin. He was wearing a Cleveland Indians baseball cap.

"We should hurry," he scolded. "I've been buzzing you for about ten minutes." Then he directed Ned to a car even worse than his own. It was an old Ford Maverick painted in a snazzy-for-the-early-seventies blue-on-blue two-tone and Ned had to admit it was in remarkable shape considering its age. It had been well cared for every day of its long life.

Once in the car, the Mayan started taking a familiar route out of town to the ranch house. He asked Ned, "Are you a driver or a shooter?"

"Driver," Ned said without hesitation, though in fact, he did not know that he was either. He just knew he did not want to be a shooter.

"They tell me I'm a shooter," El Chango II said with a chuckle. "But I had never picked up a gun in my life before this month. A machete I can use, but a gun . . ."

"It's easy," Ned said. "Just point and shoot."

"Easy for you to say, growing up in America."

"What do you mean?"

"I've seen your movies and TV shows," he said. "Everyone carries a gun and there are shoot-outs all the time . . . I honestly don't know how any of you people manage to stay alive for very long."

"It's not really like that."

"Sure it is."

"No, it's not," Ned said. "I never even saw a gun until I joined a gang."

"See? You were jumped into a gang!" said the Mayan. "Who was it? The Bloods? The Cripples? The Cosa Nostras?"

"Nothing like that," Ned grinned. "And I wasn't forced to join anything." Then he thought for a minute. "What about you? You talk like I'm a gangster and you're an upstanding member of the community. In case you haven't noticed, we're working together."

"Did they kidnap you?"

"As a matter of fact, they did, smart guy."

El Chango II looked genuinely shocked. "Really? I thought you were some kind of boss or something."

"Nope, kidnapped at a fake police checkpoint," Ned told him. "Some guys dressed as Federales were shaking me down for bribes, then there was a gun battle and the next thing I know, I was being brought to the ranch house and I have been working for these guys ever since."

"You got kidnapped to sell . . . not even sell, just deliver . . . weed?" El Chango II said to him. "An American? Working as a delivery boy in Mexico? That makes sense to you?"

"Nothing down here makes sense," Ned snapped back, but he got the other man's point. It was an unlikely story, so he quickly changed the subject. "What about you, tough guy?"

"Some guys from up here took over my family's avocado farm to grow weed; kicked us off. Well, actually they offered us jobs as pickers and dryers, but my old man was way too proud to allow that—so they shot him and hung his body up in the town square as a warning to others. It looked like a really good time to get out of Chiapas, so me and a bunch of my friends took a bus to the capital. Nobody would hire us Mayans for anything, even to push a broom, so we kept going north, hoping to cross into Texas. They say you can work there the same hour you show up."

"Then what happened?"

"Got on a bus in Zacatecas that was stopped by some masked men with guns on a deserted stretch of road. They made everyone get out; put the girls and young women in one truck, young men in another, left the old people behind. I saw the men with guns pay the driver."

"Sounds like they have a going concern," Ned told him, thinking that he now knew of at least one source for the endless supply of girls at the ranch house. "A business that never runs out of supply or customers."

"Yeah, that's what I thought too," El Chango II said. "Never saw the women again, but they split the men into two groups—one group was supposed to carry product over the border and the other was to train as *sicarios*; you know, killers."

"Why didn't you go over the border," Ned asked. "Sounds exactly like what you wanted."

"I did ask," the Mayan sighed. "But they only wanted guys with families, so that they had an incentive for them to come back. They knew that if I crossed, I would be picking strawberries in Texas and forgetting they ever existed."

"So because you didn't have a family, they gave you a gun and trained you to be an assassin?"

"Yeah, they gave me a wooden gun at first—just to get used to it—then a real one."

"So," Ned paused. "Have you shot anyone?"

El Chango II studied Ned's face. Satisfied that he was not a boss or someone else who would get him in trouble for answering honestly, he laughed. "Nah, I went on a job once and just fired in the air," he said. "Nobody noticed and when they saw my clip was empty, they all bought me drinks."

"Who were you shooting at?"

"Don't know. They don't tell me. They just put me in a van with some other guys, took us to a big house, and told us to shoot anyone we did not recognize."

Ned laughed. "Very professional."

"Actually, the other guys were," the Mayan said with a shrug. "They were very organized, almost like it was a military operation. I guess they just brought me along for laughs. What about you?"

"Me?" Ned was surprised that El Chango II wanted to know about him. His own life seemed boring in comparison, but he assumed he was exotic to the man and didn't want to disappoint him. "All I do is distribute weed around the neighborhood."

"What? And you have a house like that?" He seemed shocked, maybe a bit angry.

"Yeah," Ned said sheepishly.

"They have plans for you, buddy."

"That's what everyone tells me."

* * *

"He's not here," Meloni told Tovar and O'Malley. "Although I appreciate your diligence in checking out every angle of every clue, I really don't think we're gonna find Aiken in the tri-state area, the mid-Atlantic, or anywhere around here. Let's face it: the perp has fled the scene. So where is he?"

"We have to find the bike," O'Malley said. She was still disappointed that the bike she went to go look at had not turned out to be Aiken's. "He loved the bike. He bought it when he had no money. He restored it—to show-stopping quality—even though he made just a hair better than minimum wage. And after he sold it, he stole it back with a great deal of danger to his own personal safety. You find the bike, and I'm sure Aiken will be close by, trying to get it back."

"We can't find the bike," Meloni pointed out. "Nobody seems to have seen it. Unless you can provide something to make me think it still exists, we have nothing."

"Sure, but we also have to find the girlfriend in Moldova," said Tovar. "Aiken is a sucker for the opposite sex. Not that he's a skirt chaser, just a sucker. Didn't he risk everything he had for the little girl he met hours before? Didn't he bring his girlfriend along when he tried to get over the border into Canada? The guy is a romantic to an almost ridiculous fault. Not exactly your grade-A gangster tough guy. Get to the girl or the girls, and you get to him."

"Well, the little girl doesn't know anything, or won't talk. And the girlfriend is somewhere in Eastern Europe—if she hasn't escaped from her hellhole of a country again," Meloni said. "So we can't find her."

"But if we could . . ."

"Yeah, if we could find the girlfriend, if we could find the bike, everything would be great," Meloni said. "But we haven't found anything. Until we do, we have to work with what we have. Tovar, you keep investigating Andersson, Hawkridge, and the guy who bought the Indian off Aiken. O'Malley, talk with the CIA, see what we can get on the girlfriend. Keep an eye on the little girl and just find out whatever you can."

They both agreed. Pressure from Harrison and open criticism from other officers had made Meloni even more desperate to get to the bottom of Kuzik's murder. Not only would it shut his detractors up once and for all, it might also get him out of Philadelphia.

* * *

When Ned and El Chango II arrived, the ranch house was buzzing with activity. There were more SUVs and pickup trucks than usual, along with a pair of cube vans Ned had never seen before. Both of them were decorated with business names and logos—one for a fruit-and-vegetable supplier, the other a home-electronics retailer. Men were everywhere. Some were dressed as soldiers, others as Federales, and a few as Sonora state police. But most were in jeans.

It appeared as though the hard work of loading the trucks was over and that the men were waiting for further instruction. Ned could tell they were nervous by how many of them were pacing about. El Chango II found a parking spot, and the two walked toward the house.

They were greeted by El Ratón, who spoke only to Ned. "Ah, Espagueti! You will be with El Martillo, in the white Suburban," he said, pointing to a giant truck that had men around it. "Since you are American, I expect you know how to use this," he said, handing him an AR-15 assault rifle.

Ned had never touched that kind of gun before, but was pretty sure he could find the safety and the trigger—or at least ask someone how it worked. "What about him?" he asked.

"Who?" the big man answered, confused.

"El Chango," Ned said, pointing at his driver.

El Ratón looked at Ned as though he was crazy then, glanced derisively at El Chango II. "Who cares?" he laughed then walked slowly toward another SUV.

Ned went over to El Martillo and his crew. They acknowledged him with nods. "We're just waiting for the order," Martillo told him.

Ned nodded and asked what his job was.

"Just ride in the back and shoot at anyone you don't recognize." He felt much less nervous now that he realized that they did not expect much of him. It appeared that his participation in this mission was more of a rite of passage for him than anything of strategic import for the organization.

"I don't recognize most of these guys," Ned said with a chuckle.

"Yeah, and I bet we all look alike, too," said one of the other men in his team.

Ned could do nothing but smile. He felt that anything else would have invited violence.

Breaking the tension, Martillo told Ned only to shoot at anyone who was pointing a gun at him and told the guy who spoke to him, La Lágrima, that he could be included in that group. Ned laughed, La Lágrima did not.

Martillo's cell phone rang. He answered with a few okays, snapped it shut, and told the guys to get into the trucks. The giant SUV he instructed Ned to get in had three rows of seats. The driver looked to be Mayan and was unarmed. The guy in the passenger seat was dressed as a Federale and carried an AR-15 like Ned's. Ned guessed he was a sharpshooter. Ned himself was sandwiched between two guys with AK-47s in the second row and Martillo was in the back row with two other guys who appeared to be armed only with handguns.

Theirs was the third in a convoy that took the Cuerta highway east out of Nogales, and was waved through two separate police checkpoints. As the city shrank behind them, Ned looked out at what appeared to be endless rolling mountains and hills covered with nothing but sand, dirt, and the occasional cactus or scrub. This land was not good enough for any type of farming or even ranching and so was just left to itself. Other than the mounds of garbage every few yards, it looked as though humans had abandoned the area long ago. The road seemed to take the path of least resistance, snaking around boulders and hills, making every mile toward the destination seem like five in actual driving.

The drive took hours and the men began to loosen up once they were deep into the desert. One of the third-row guys pulled some water bottles out of a cooler in the back and handed them out. The men put their guns at their sides and started talking. None addressed Ned directly, but he figured out what they were all doing.

The cube vans were full of drugs, mostly coke, some meth, and some weed. The rest of the vehicles were full of gunmen for protection. The plan was simple. There was a point on the highway that was just a hundred or so feet from the U.S. border. On the other side of the border was Coronado National Forest. Their convoy would meet up with a bus full of men and women whose job would be to cross the border with backpacks full of drugs. At the same time as the cube vans disgorged the drugs, they would be filled up with cash and perhaps weapons from their contacts in Arizona. If they were intercepted by the Americans—the DEA or border patrol—or by the Mexican military, the plan was to run. But if it was the Federales, the state police, or another cartel, they were instructed to shoot their way to freedom.

Ned could tell they had arrived when he saw about two dozen poor-looking people milling about outside a dilapidated old bus. The border was indeed close and consisted of an ancient wire fence. There were three visible breaches in the quarter mile or so around the bus. The convoy surrounded the bus and the more senior members from the ranch-house crew instructed the bus passengers to unload the cube vans and put the drugs in their backpacks. They would then cross over the border in groups of three or four. At about the same time, other operatives would return with backpacks full of U.S. currency or weapons, which they would dutifully load into the now-empty cube vans. Once finished, they would be directed to get on the bus so that the cycle could be repeated.

Sitting on the ground with his back up against the Suburban, Ned marveled at how efficient the process was, when he heard the sound of engines. He wasn't sure if it was more of his crew, the cops, or another gang. Instinctively, he looked over at Martillo, the authority figure, who was smoking a joint about six feet away from him. Noticing that Ned was looking, Martillo took a huge drag and grinned at Ned as he held the smoke in his lungs. Ned was waiting for him to exhale when a hole opened up in Martillo's head. Later, in his dreams, Ned would remember seeing light through the hole. Blood and brain tissue flew from Martillo's head onto Ned's shirt.

Ned leaped to his feet. He could hear the shots now. Along with the *budda-budda* of AK-47s and the *zing-zing-zing* of the AR-15s, he could sense, but not quite hear, the report of a hard-core sniper rifle, maybe even a Barrett.

He ran. People—shooters, drivers, and drug mules— were running and falling all around him. He could see vehicles shot full of holes, but he could not see who was doing the shooting. He ran, not knowing what to do. The driver's door of one of the cube vans was open. He leaped inside. Realizing that he was in a huge target, he felt for the key in the ignition. It was there. He turned it and the old Chevy V8 eagerly came to life. Against every instinct he had, Ned sat up straight and stepped on the gas. He turned the van toward the highway and had to stomp on the brake pedal to avoid killing two men, one of whom was badly injured and being dragged by the other out of the line of fire. Ned stared at them, then came to his senses and opened the passenger door. The *snap-snap* of the guns became *boom-booms*. The healthier man dragged the hurt man into the cab then leaped in. He didn't say anything, just slammed the door. Ned stood on the gas pedal. The cube van lurched onto the highway, the back wheels caught the pavement, and the big truck sped down the road like it was flung from a slingshot.

Ned never looked back. The two men in the cab with him were panicking. Blood was dripping from the neck of the injured man into the foot well of the cube van. The other man, confused and overwhelmed, was praying and crying. He pulled off his necklace with a pendant of what looked to Ned like the Grim Reaper, and pushed it onto the other guy's chest chanting something Ned didn't understand.

Twenty miles from the attack, Ned regained his wits. He knew that no amount of praying to whomever this guy was praying was going to help the bleeding man. He pulled the cube van over to the side of the road, leaped out of the driver's side door and ran around the front of the van. He opened the passenger door, used his left arm to push the uninjured man aside, and took a close look at the other. He had a huge gash on his neck, but it hadn't affected his windpipe, his jugular, or his carotid. It was a flesh wound. Ned took off his shirt and pressed it against the wound then instructed the other guy to keep up the pressure, and went back to the driver's seat.

He drove. He just drove not knowing where to go. But the Cuerta highway only goes one place. He blasted through a police checkpoint at seventy-five miles per hour. He heard a few gunshots, but nobody chased him. He made it to Nogales. That's when it occurred to him. He had no place to go. No place other than the ranch house.

They were among the first ones back. There were a couple of SUVs and one pickup truck already there. All the vehicles had holes in them and either smoke or steam was coming from under the hood of the pickup. As soon as he got out of the cube van, Ned ran to the group of men gathered in front of the veranda. "This man needs to go to a hospital!" he shouted. Without a word, one of the men ran to the cube van and helped move the injured man to one of the SUVs, then took off toward the city.

Nobody else spoke. There was some muttering about who'd been hit and who hadn't. But nobody wanted to talk with Ned. In fact, they studiously avoided even eye contact with him. As the hours passed, more and more vehicles came back, often with badly injured men. Still nobody talked to Ned. Finally, he saw El Chango II emerge from one of the SUVs. Ned rushed over to greet him, but slowed down when he saw all the others stare.

"Good to see you made it," he said.

"Yeah, you too, man," the Mayan replied. "But I wouldn't want to be in your shoes. Some of the guys think this was your fault. I heard them talking. Some say you are DEA, others say you are in with the Sinaloans or Los Zetas. Some just say you are bad luck to have around. I would lay low if I were you. Don't do anything to draw attention to yourself."

Before Ned could answer, El Ratón burst from the ranch house with two men brandishing AK-47s. He stopped at the edge of the veranda and shouted as loud as he could: "Attention El Espagueti! The boss will see you. Stay with these men until a ride can be arranged."

A murmur rose from the crowd. Somebody cheered.

Chapter Seven

Agent Bob Fernandez of the CIA laughed into the phone. Tovar had been inquiring with the agency's office in Moldova about Aiken's former girlfriend, Daniela Eminescu, who had been deported back to the country. O'Malley had been assigned the task, but when she received no answer after repeated attempts, Tovar, who had friends in the CIA, tried his hand. He was actually surprised that they had not gotten back to him. "You were actually serious about that?" Fernandez asked incredulously. "I mean, sure, we can try, but to find something like that would be almost impossible."

Tovar was surprised. CIA agents didn't normally act that way. Usually it was all rah-rah, by-the-book optimism from them. This guy was acting like he worked in the DMV or some other government office. "What's the problem?" he asked.

"Moldova is the poorest, worst-run, most corrupt country in all of Europe," Fernandez answered. "Humans are its main export. The cops there are paid less than janitors, government officials are all mobbed up. The most we can do here is keep an eye on who's paying whom. I'm just grateful that there's no serious Islamic fundamentalist movement here."

The FBI agent pressed. "That's not what I heard," he said. "Isn't Moldova how you guys get sophisticated Russian weaponry for 'research purposes'? Don't I remember something about a shipment of MiG-29s that ended up in D.C.?"

The CIA man laughed again. "I don't know where you get your information," he said. "But that's hardly an FBI issue."

"But the Aiken investigation is," Tovar said. "And a major lead brings it to Moldova."

"I am aware of that, but we are totally swamped here and get literally no help from the locals," Fernandez said. "I wish we could do more."

"I know you are aware of the gravity of this murder investigation; in fact, the murder of a fellow agent," Tovar said. "I do hope you will put appropriate resources on the case."

Fernandez sighed. "I've been looking at the file while we've been talking and I think there's another problem," he said. "The name she gave you and Immigration was Eminescu, right?"

"Yeah, why's that a problem?"

"Well, Mihail Eminescu is kind of a national hero around here; a poet, he's kind of a big deal," Fernandez said. "Everything is named after him here, streets, museums, libraries, parks, restaurants, you name it."

"So it's a common name; is that it?"

"No, quite the opposite, nobody has it anymore," Fernandez answered. "That she told you her name was Eminescu is kind of like if she told you her name was Shakespeare or Voltaire or something like that. It's obviously a fake. And since she was arrested and deported without any official papers, all you have for her identity is her word."

"But we have a description, dozens of photos . . ."

"This isn't New York City," Fernandez said. "This is old-school Eastern Europe—everyone here is from the same ethnic group. Hell, I think three-quarters of them are cousins at the very least. Your pictures, your description—they should narrow it down to about a quarter-million people or so. That is, if she's still in the country. The borders here are imaginary in some places. And nobody is ever still here if they can find a way to get out. This woman you're talking about seems smart—or at least cunning—enough to have left Dodge by now."

"I'm beginning to see your point, but if something turns up . . ."

Fernandez chuckled. "Hey, something is always turning up in this inbred pigsty," he said sympathetically. "Did I tell you that the country was actually named after some guy's dog?"

* * *

Ned was trembling. He knew these guys were serious. In between two tough-looking guys with AK-47s and in front of two more guys with handguns in the third row of the giant SUV, all he could think about was the guy he saw get blinded in Russia because he was caught stealing from the mafia. He knew the Mexican cartels had a habit of torturing prisoners for answers or sometimes just for show, to threaten the competition. The guys at the ranch house used to watch them do it on YouTube and other video-sharing sites until the videos were eventually taken down. The men would laugh and laugh as some poor guy would be beaten, burned, and cut. He'd seen men and boys have their fingers, ears, lips, and other parts sliced off, literally disassembled on camera. The images from those videos ran over and over in his head as the Suburban made its way into Del Rosario, one of Nogales's better but not great neighborhoods.

The SUV pulled up, not in front of the massive estate or mansion that Ned had expected after seeing how Russian crime bosses live, but into the driveway of a comfortable but unprepossessing townhouse that would not have been out of place in Tucson or El Paso. The men made no effort to hide their guns when they escorted Ned in.

Inside, the house was typical of the ostentatious decor Ned knew drug bosses appreciated. There were gold weapons, statues of various dangerous animals, and original oil paintings of heroic- or at least masculine-looking figures. But dominating all of it was a gold and jeweled figurine of the Grim Reaper portrayed as an angel. It was an image Ned had seen before—a humbler version of it had hung around the neck of the injured foot soldier he'd rescued in the ambush—and he had noticed that many of the Mexicans seemed to revere it.

Ned was pushed down to a couch and told to wait. After an agonizing four or five minutes, a man walked in. Ned was shocked. It was the long-haired man he had spoken with about his AK-47 on the ranch-house veranda. Against his will, Ned began to shake again. The man looked at him, grinned, spread his arms in a mock shrug and said: "Surprised?" Then he sent the guards out of the room.

Once they had left, the boss smiled again and said: "Don't worry, man, you're not in trouble. You're here to be praised." He lit a cigar, and offered Ned one.

Ned begged off. "Honestly, I didn't think I had done anything wrong." It was all he could think to say, even though he knew he had run from the gunfight rather than shoot.

"Wrong? Of course there were some losses, but what could have happened would have been far worse. Trust me, I have seen this happen many, many times before," the boss smirked dramatically. "But what you did, you think I want to punish you? Are you kidding? You bravely drove a cube van full of my cash—maybe $6 million, maybe even more— back to regional headquarters and saved another man's life. A man you didn't even know. A man who—I am ashamed to say—suspected and perhaps even hated you. If anything, you should be rewarded."

Ned was beginning to regroup. "Okay, then why did everyone at the ranch house want to kill me?"

"They are—as a group—very suspicious," the boss said, "and I will also admit that many of them are not very well educated. They don't have the tolerance and confidence that worldliness has given men such as you and me. When something bad happens, they immediately look for someone to blame. Someone, anyone, other than themselves. You look different than them, so it had to be you. The *changos* are also different, but our men don't respect them enough to fear or even blame them." He sat in a chair behind a desk facing the couch. "Besides, you are American. These guys, the whole world, they blame everything on you—the weather even."

"But you're not like them. Are you even from Mexico?"

The boss smiled and rubbed his face in frustration. "Ah, but you make the same mistake they do. Just as the Mexicans think all Americans just want to take advantage of them, you, an American, think all Mexicans are uneducated and uncultured. These beliefs, what you call stereotypes, may bring comfort and a feeling of superiority among the uneducated, but they can also be dangerous." He stood. "Don't think these Sonoran hicks and wannabes represent my entire country. In fact, Mexico has an old and proud culture with countless achievements. I have two master's degrees myself—would have gotten a doctorate, but couldn't stand the politics at the universities. And I am worth several billion of your American dollars."

"I'm sorry, I didn't mean to offend."

"It's quite alright," the man smiled again. "I understand that your time in Mexico has not exposed you to our more impressive people and places." The man approached Ned. "Allow me to change that by introducing myself," he said, extending his hand. "I am Jesús Bravo Meléndez."

"Better known as Poco Loco?"

Bravo sighed and sat on his desk. "Yes, sadly. But it is a necessary part of doing business. Like any business, it's all about branding. People need to know who you are; you need an image that sticks with them."

"And you picked a dead clown?"

"A dead, but universally beloved clown," Poco Loco smiled. "It is a sad fact of life in this region that the only way to build respect is through fear."

"And people are afraid of the clown?"

"No, not in and of himself. Not at all. But it's a tried-and-true psychological trick. It was one of your more astute Hollywood directors—I think it may have been John Carpenter—who said something very inspirational to me," Poco Loco explained. "From the familiar comes real fear—to see a strange man threaten you with a blood-stained knife is scary, but to see your mother threaten you with a blood-stained knife—well, that is truly terrifying. Everybody grew up with the clown, they loved the clown, they felt for him when his daughter was killed, they wept when he killed himself."

"I see your point," Ned said, chilled to the bone. "So what do you need me for?"

"I don't *need* anyone," he said sharply, then sighed. "Allow me to explain. You know what we do here? Obviously, it's more than just dropping off tiny bags of weed to a bunch of peasants."

Ned nodded.

"Years ago, after we stopped letting the Colombians push us around," Poco Loco continued, "some people here in Mexico started making ridiculous amounts of money; I must admit—with all modesty—that I am one of them. All the bosses had a working agreement, but then things changed. Calderón and his arrogant government—blind to how truly powerful we had become—attempted to put us down, and then that stupid asshole from Sinaloa, El Chapo (how I curse his name), started to take more than his fair share, breaking the detente. Since then, everyone has been fighting everyone. Nobody wants to give up, so its gets more violent, more corrupt, more insidious."

"It like the whole country is in a gang war."

Poco Loco smiled. "I like to think of it more as a civil war."

"Really? You want to have the country run by drug dealers?"

Poco Loco did not look offended at Ned's accusation. "All the great countries came from rebellions led by so-called criminals. Look at your own, a bunch of rich men who refused to pay their taxes. Look at Israel, or South Africa. Mandela spent twenty-seven years in jail for a fire bombing, now he is an international symbol of peace."

"I know your men well," Ned said. "None of them are thinking like Mandela."

"They don't have to, and neither did Mandela's men, I might add. You don't understand, we have lived for countless generations under a corrupt and brutal regime and it needs to be replaced. If we must sell some coke to your people to finance that, so be it. You can afford it."

"And hang people from overpasses and drive gold-plated Mercedes SUVs . . ."

Poco Loco smiled. "But you don't know what it's like to have power; I mean, real power," he said. "All of my life, I've seen these guys, I know them well. They realize they can do whatever they want, whatever they ever wanted and they become confused. Some of them, they go crazy for sex. They do everything to anything that walks, but it always ends up in deeper frustration as their imaginations are very limited. They are looking for the young love they feel they missed out on, but they never, ever find it. In fact, what they are chasing just gets farther and farther away no matter how hard they try. It makes them crazy with frustration. Usually they turn to violence (although some start there); they get a love for killing. It becomes a love of theirs to watch people die. But unless you are a particular type of psychopath, killing becomes boring, it's so . . . so . . . how do I say this? Anti-climactic. You get used to it. To understand all of this, many turn to their own drugs and that never ends well. These men, they are no better than the thieves and liars who govern us. And, like them, they will fall victim to their own excesses and moral depravity."

"And your men won't?"

"Not with me in command they won't," Poco Loco said confidently. "All movements require a charismatic leader. Once we are in charge, things will be better, much better."

Ned, aware that he was in little danger as he seemed to be part of Poco Loco's master plan, changed the subject. "What can I do?" he asked.

"It must have been obvious to a fellow man of the world from the start I had some plans for you," he said. "I trust the men at the ranch house treated you well?"

Ned nodded.

"Good, good, I instructed them to treat you as they would me," he said. "When I came to check on you, you seemed well, but somewhat trapped—that's why you got the house."

"Thank you."

Poco Loco smiled. "Well, you're not going to need it anymore," he said. "It's a case of relocation . . . a transfer, if you will."

"Relocation?"

"Yes, and you will be happy about where it is—Nogales!"

"I'm already in Nogales."

"No, you did not hear me, my friend, not Nogales, but Nogales." He did pronounce the second one slightly differently, less Spanish. "Not Nogales, Sonora, but Nogales, Arizona."

Ned could feel the blood rush from his face. "I can't go back to the United States."

"Yes, yes you can—just don't get in trouble up there." Poco Loco looked dismissive. "Pay cash for everything, drive the speed limit, don't get in fights, wear a golf shirt . . . there will be no problem."

"American cops are not like Mexican cops."

"Oh, I know, they are harder to bribe and harder to kill," Poco Loco laughed. "But all cops can be bribed or disposed of. Don't worry. You will be well armed with both money and weapons. Besides, they have to worry about warrants and probable cause and all of that. They are no problem. And you will have men."

"Men?"

Poco Loco shrugged. "I have a small organization based in Nogales," he said, again using his American pronunciation. "They are called the Cossacks."

"Bikers?"

"Why are you surprised?" Poco Loco asked. "You are a biker, my friend (yes, I know exactly who you are), and you can't ever leave it completely. I know you, Mr. Aiken, and your type."

Ned sighed. "I've heard of the Cossacks," he said. "They move a lot of product; have a reputation for violence; and really, really hate the Hells Angels."

Poco Loco smiled again. "I'm afraid with them and the Hells Angels, their differences come from more than just business, but that won't be a problem," he said. "Because of the Cossacks and a major infiltration by law enforcement, the Hells Angels are very weak in Arizona at the moment and I don't see them fixing that right away." He made no effort to hide the pride on his face. "The Cossacks are very much in charge up there and there is essentially no violence."

"Why me? What's my job?"

"My friends in Arizona like to talk. I have heard you are experienced and organized, we need that up there, and . . ."

"And?"

"You're white," Poco Loco said with a shrug. "People like to buy product from people who look like them—you wouldn't go selling weed on the streets of Harlem, would you? Lots of buyers, just not for you. And the Mexicans that are up in Arizona? They have no money. We need to move to the *gueros*, that's where the money is. Besides, we have enough Mexicans addicted already. I have no desire that more of my people should fall prey to drugs."

"But I thought the Cossacks were white."

"Depends on the area," Poco Loco said. "In most of California, they are about fifty-fifty and it works very well, but in some places they are all Mexican—and that works less well. In places like Nevada, they have to sell through the Crips and even less savory groups."

"So I'm going to be on the street?" Ned asked.

"No, no, no," said Poco Loco in a tone Ned was sure was supposed to be reassuring. "You will be the president; you won't be anywhere near the street. The customers don't need to deal directly with you; they just know that you're there."

Ned put his face in his hands. Poco Loco's reassurances did not fill him with confidence. He knew that going back to the United States, let alone living there, was dangerous. But he also knew that Mexico was now far more dangerous, because it would be impossible to refuse Poco Loco and walk out of the townhouse alive. "So . . . let's get started," he said with all the enthusiasm he could muster.

* * *

Dudley Weise could not believe his luck. He had been sifting through stolen and recovered motorcycle reports when he struck pay dirt. Just outside the town of Sahuarita, Arizona, a man had been killed when his motorcycle had been destroyed by a semi. While the other officers were looking for living people's motorcycles, Weise thought it would be prudent also to look at dead people's. The truck driver claimed not to have seen the man he hit, who was stopped for reasons unknown, probably—the local cops guessed— engine trouble due to the bike's age.

The dead man's name was Harry Lucas. A local magnate of sorts, Lucas was probably the richest man in town on the strength of a business that made custom air-conditioning systems for commercial and industrial properties. But the local police had some questions. A positive ID was made on Lucas's body, and his friends and family said that he rode the bike frequently, but the cops quickly found that it was not registered to him. The bike's VIN had been rather sloppily filed off, and the license plate belonged to a Mark Troutman, a former employee of Lucas's who been killed by a drunk driver while on a trip to the Dominican Republic. The plates identified the bike as a 2009 Suzuki Hayabusa, a supersports bike that had almost nothing in common with the ancient Indian Lucas had been riding.

The local cops were pretty sure Lucas was riding a stolen bike, though they couldn't be sure if he was aware of that or not. Considering his reputation as the most successful man in town, it was hard for them to believe he'd risk it all for an old bike. And after checking for stolen Indians in Arizona and finding none, they sent a request to the FBI. As soon as he finished reading the report, Weise printed it and ran toward Tovar's cubicle.

"I think I found the bike!" he said.

"Aiken's Indian? Where?"

"Arizona."

* * *

A few of Poco Loco's girls had bought Ned some clothes for his new career—khaki shorts and a lime-green Nike golf shirt. "White-guy uniform," Ned thought to himself. Poco Loco had assigned Ned a handler who would take care of him until he was sent over the border. The handler—Hilario, better known by the ranch-house gang as "El Seinfeld"—wasn't a bad guy by any means, but he had an annoying habit of laughing and giggling at anything that anyone—even, maybe particularly, himself—said. The fact that Ned was an American sneaking over the border never failed to make him erupt into laughter whenever it occurred to him. And it did, over and over again.

He had taken Ned out for some fancy meals and had given him his border-crossing kit. Ned would have no weapons and only a token amount of cash until he could hook up with the Cossacks on the other side. His story, if he was intercepted, was that he was a tourist and had gotten lost while bird-watching. They supplied him with binoculars and a field guide to the birds of western North America. He was given a wallet that had identification and credit cards identifying him as Ian Wuerth. The picture in the driver's license and other cards had been altered to look like Ned. It was a professional-looking job, but Hilario had warned him they were only good for Border Patrol and not cops, because the cops would run the cards through their computers while the Border Patrol guys would just give them the eyeball test. Ned asked who Wuerth was. "Just some gringo asshole partying down at Cancún," Hilario said. "In the old days when you took a wallet, you'd grab the money and throw the rest away. But now the identification is worth more than the money." Ned realized that some guy from Kenosha, Wisconsin, getting his wallet stolen in Cancún would not be at the top of the news for Border Patrol or the police in Arizona, so it made him feel a little less uneasy. Along with the wallet was a card key from the Doubletree Resort in Tucson.

When it came time, the girls wished Ned luck and one of them, Luz, kissed him on the cheek. In his heavily customized pickup, Hilario drove Ned down the Cuerta highway back to the spot where the drug caravan had been attacked, *narcocorridas* blasting from the many speakers inside the cab. Realizing that Ned was nervous about the spot, Hilario told him that the Sinaloans had been dealt with and they were perfectly safe in this area.

"Dealt with?"

Hilario's eyebrows went up and he started laughing again. "Yeah, the boss had a conversation with the army commander here—whatsisname, Gutierrez or whatever," he said. "His boys and some Federales rounded up a bunch of their shooters, threw 'em in jail."

"Really?"

"Yeah," he said between giggles. "But they'll be broken out in a few days."

"How do you know?"

"Escajeda, the warden, is in Sinaloa's hands—just like Gutierrez is in ours," he said. "He owes them a favor. He'll keep them for a couple of weeks, go on vacation, and then when he's away, truckloads of armed men will show up and free the Sinaloas without a shot being fired. Happens all the time. It helps maintain the balance."

"What will happen to the warden?"

"Depends," Hilario actually stopped giggling for a second while he was thinking. "If the investigator is aligned with us, he'll lose his job, maybe go to jail for a little while, but if he's aligned with them, then nothing will happen— there will be, as we say here, 'insufficient evidence' to move on with the investigation."

"What if the investigator is not on either side?"

That question made Hilario laugh harder than Ned had ever seen before. He continued to laugh until he stopped the truck by the side of the road. He pointed at the fence. "Pick your hole," he said, laughing. "They all go to the same place."

As they had discussed, Ned would cross the border and then walk down the trail until he came across an old bathtub full of water. The bathtub had been placed over a natural spring in a clearing and was always full of fresh, relatively clean water. Because of this, it was frequented by hikers. When he got there, he would be greeted by some Cossacks dressed as hikers. They would take him back to the city with them and set him up with a place to live and a vehicle. Ned took the backpack Hilario had prepared for him. Along with the bird book and binoculars, it was full of water bottles. Hilario had pointed out with pride that they had labels in English to prevent the Border Patrol from becoming too suspicious.

They said their good-byes and Ned ran to the nearest breach in the fence. He had to duck and contort a bit to get through it, but was otherwise fine. There was no mistaking the trail. As soon as he was over the border, he encountered a mountain of trash, most of it the discarded packages of decongestant pills, used in the manufacture of methamphetamine. The trail itself consisted of sand trampled by thousands of human feet.

Ned walked for about twenty minutes before he realized he was back in the United States. The trash left behind by the border-crossers was behind him and he was now on a trail cared for by the National Forest Service. It was, he had to admit, quite beautiful and serene. It actually prompted him to put his water bottle back in his backpack when he emptied it, rather than just throw it to the ground.

He walked for almost an hour, following the trail markers, when he came to the bathtub. In a clearing surrounded by a few sparse trees, the old white tub stood out. Ned could hear the water from the spring even though someone had covered the tub with wooden boards to protect the water. He wasn't alone there, but it wasn't his contacts. As Ned sat and rested on a rock facing the tub, he saw that a quartet of somewhat older hikers was enjoying the trail as well. One of them, a big man with what Ned thought was a "porn star" mustache, approached him and asked "*sprechen sie deutsch?*" Ned said he didn't, and the man apologized for his poor English. To discourage further conversation, Ned took out his book and his binoculars and started looking around aimlessly. The German guy backed off and his group soon left.

Ned was reading about roadrunners when he heard some men approaching. There were three of them and they did not move with the slightest indication that they wanted to escape detection. Although they were dressed like he was, Ned had no problem identifying them as bikers, or at least as bad guys. All three were Mexican, steroided-up bodybuilder types. All of them had goatees and were covered in tattoos. Two of them had shaved heads and the other had long black hair in a ponytail.

"You our guy?" the ponytailed one, the obvious leader, asked.

"I think so," Ned answered. "You the Cossacks?"

"Some of 'em," the big man said. "Who sent you?"

"Poco Loco."

"What's your name?"

"Ian, but you can call me Crash."

"Well Mr. Crash, our pickup is about a half-hour's walk that way." The man extended his hand, but the other two did not. "I'm Duane, but they call me Weasel, these guys are Speedy and El Borracho." Both men nodded coolly in acknowledgment. As a group these three seemed far from warm, even by biker standards. "You have water?" Weasel asked. Ned acknowledged that he did, and the group started walking after Speedy, who was already several yards down the trail.

* * *

When the lab determined that the bike Harry Lucas had died on was in all likelihood the one formerly owned by—and allegedly stolen by—Ned Aiken, Meloni called a meeting of his team. Weise was invited, but Tovar instructed him to stay in the background. Interns tended to be seen and not heard at this kind of meeting.

Tovar admitted that he was temporarily confused. Because Aiken's cover identity in the witness protection program, Steadman, came from Gila, Arizona, he believed for a moment that Aiken was going home to visit friends. But then he wondered why Aiken had gone to Arizona. A very "red" state, Arizona had a few libertarian and even anti-government types who make hiding an identity part of their philosophy, but it was nothing like Idaho or Montana where that kind of thing is commonplace. If he was going to hide in plain sight, Arizona was not a great choice.

O'Malley pointed out that Arizona had a large Native American population and that testimony from the Sons of Satan trial indicated that many members (including Aiken) had close ties to Natives back in the Midwest.

Tovar countered that the Navajos, Yaquis, and Zunis of Arizona had little in common with the Mohawks the Sons were dealing with and had almost no contact with either group. In fact, the Arizona Native groups registered as just tiny blips on the organized-crime radar, while the Mohawks were more like a tsunami. It was truly unlikely, he opined, that Aiken would have any friends among the Natives in the southwest.

O'Malley could not help but agree, and introduced the idea of outlaw biker gangs. "There are no Sons, Outlaws,

Lawbreakers or, despite the proximity to Texas, Bandidos chapters there," she said. "Although any or all of those clubs will ride through the state to get to Las Vegas or Southern California, none have any feet on the ground there."

Tovar asked who the main biker presence was. "Reflecting the demographics, history, and culture of the state, it was strongly Hells Angels territory for several decades," she said. "They were the top dogs in organized crime there until . . ."

"Until Jaybird Dobyns and the ATF's Operation Black Biscuit knocked them down," Meloni interrupted.

"Exactly," O'Malley continued a beat later. "After the ATF infiltration, the Hells Angels were in terrible shape in Arizona—bikers had to be imported from California just to keep the chapters there alive."

"So who's filled the vacuum?" Tovar asked.

"That's where it gets complicated," O'Malley answered. "The logical successors would appear to have been the Mongols, the Hells Angels' sworn enemies who have done a great job stealing territory from them in Cali, but a federal court judgment against them has forbidden them to expand. And they have abided by that."

"And the Bandidos?" asked Meloni.

"They've been severely set back by arrests and a massacre in Canada," she said. "And they have given up a lot of territory to the Mexicans."

"The Mexicans?" Tovar asked.

"Yeah, drugs have been coming from Mexico since forever, but traditionally, they have used the bikers to move them to primarily non-Hispanic communities," she said. "But they have been gaining in confidence and have begun retailing locally and moving product to other primarily Hispanic gangs as far away as Seattle, Toronto, and Boston. As in Texas and California, the major Mexican cartels have working associations with largely Mexican gangs on this side of the border. But nothing with the clout of a Barrio Azteca or White Fence."

"Anyone else?" Meloni asked. "Anyone?"

"Not too much, the Italians have ties there, but nothing on the ground outside of Phoenix-Tempe and even there they rarely get their hands dirty," she said. "Aside from Mexicans and bikers, you still have a few crazy meth cooks, but they've mostly blown themselves up or been chased away by the bigger fish from south of the border."

Weise spoke up, hoping to stop the back-and-forth between the two senior officers. "So if Aiken has no friends in Arizona," he offered, "is there a chance that he could have slipped across the border?"

"Good point," said Tovar, who had become something of a sponsor for the intern and wanted to deflect the fact that he had broken the agency's tacit rules against interns being so bold. "There's a long and proud tradition of American felons running south of the Rio Grande to disappear."

"True," said Meloni. "But that was before Mexico turned into a war zone." He paused. "But maybe it makes no difference. Agent Tovar, you're going to Tucson. Bring your enthusiastic young friend with you."

* * *

The three Cossacks took Ned down a well-manicured trail to a road just beyond where the trees stopped. He could see sparsely grassed cattle pasture on the other side. Like many Americans, Ned made a habit of judging other people's financial success by the cars they drove, and these guys seemed to be doing fairly well. As he was coming to believe was Mexican tradition, the Chevy Tahoe SUV the men were driving was brightly painted and heavily customized.

Ned was instructed to sit in the front. After starting the engine, Weasel turned to him. "I know the Clown said you were gonna be president, but it will be in name only," he said. "We were doing fine before you got here."

Ned chuckled, surprised to find that he was happy to be out of Mexico. "I have no problem with that," he said. "I did not come here to start pushing people around or start changing things."

Weasel shifted in drive. "Then we'll all get along," he said and the men in the back laughed. "You mind *narcocorridas*?"

Ned smiled. "I've gotten used to them."

As they drove down the East Patagonia Highway past Nogales's one-strip airport, Weasel told Ned about the history of the Cossacks. "A lot of vets coming back from Vietnam had a fuck-everything attitude and joined up with bike clubs, especially the Hells," he said. "But the Hells were white-only, and refused to accept black or Latino members."

"Doesn't surprise me," Ned said, trying to sound innocent of biker culture. "I've heard of gangs like that."

Weasel smiled. "Don't bother. We know who you are, man. Poco Loco told us everything. Since you are a friend of his, you are a friend of ours," he said. "So, as I was saying, the blacks and Latinos formed their own clubs . . . like the Mongols."

"I've never heard of a black club."

"My uncle Monster, one of the founders of the Cossacks, told me there used to be a couple, but they didn't last," he explained. "I guess bikes just weren't their thing."

"So you guys still have a grudge against the Hells Angels?" Ned asked. "They have Hispanic members now. Wasn't the San Fran president Mexican? I forget his name.

"Well, he was about seventh generation, and, by the way, he was assassinated. Shot in the head on his front stoop in front of his kids."

"By the Mongols, wasn't it?"

Weasel laughed. "All I'm gonna say on that is probably—all hearsay and speculation as my lawyer likes to say," he said. "But, sure, that resentment is still there, but it's more than just that. The Hells are assholes. Everyone hates the featherheads. I mean they always move in and try to make a monopoly. They push people around, set prices, bully our dealers and friends. They suck."

"And they need to be dealt with," said one of the shaven-headed guys from the back seat.

Weasel looked at Ned and pointed his thumb at the back seat. "This is something you are going to have to deal with," he said. "Many in our membership are a bit suspicious of people they don't know—to them, you could be a Hells, an ATF, or even an FBI . . ."

"None of those guys would have me," Ned joked in an attempt to look more confident.

"But the Clown says we have to," said the other guy from the back seat.

They drove, mostly in silence aside from the stereo, to a low-slung bungalow not far from downtown. Weasel explained to Ned that he was going to share the house with Speedy for a while, until they got to know him a little better. "I know the Clown is the boss, but we have to be careful," Weasel told him. "Especially after what happened to the Hells. You understand." It was not a question.

Ned assured him he understood and went into the house with the others. After Speedy showed him around, instructing him not to use his weights set, and some terse small talk, Ned asked what he was supposed to do.

"I don't know, man," Speedy shot back. "You were brought here to be the white guy, so do white-guy stuff. Play golf, make money, don't dance. I don't care." He glared, sat on the leather couch in the middle of the living room and turned on the TV. It was one of those melodramatic Mexican soap operas that seem to be on all the time in the Southwest.

"Don't mind him," said Weasel. "He doesn't understand the long-range implications of the Clown's plan."

"He doesn't understand the word *implication*," added El Borracho.

"Like I said, I'm not here to piss anyone off," Ned offered.

"Too late," El Borracho was on a roll.

"Look, I'm the boss here and Speedy will just have to live with my decision, whether he likes it or not," Weasel said, ignoring the fact that it was indeed Poco Loco's decision that was in question. "You're here and there's nothing he can do about it—unless he wants to go over the border and tell the Clown what he thinks."

That got Speedy's attention. He shut off the TV and stood up to face the others, an act that only underlined how petulant he had been earlier. "I know, I know, if the Clown says we have to, we have to," he said. "I'm cool. Sorry, Crash."

Ned smiled. "Don't be, it's cool," he said. "We have to live together for a while so let's save the fighting until I get my own place. Keep in mind, just hours ago I was nothing but a delivery boy on the other side."

"That's what I want to hear," said Weasel, who then directed his attention to Ned. "A boy will be by later to bring you some things. Keep in mind that we can't be sure who can hear what in this house (if you know what I mean), so certain words are not to be said in English or in Spanish."

"Got it," Ned said. "Until then, I will just clean up and relax. Hey, Speedy, where do you keep the towels?"

Speedy sighed. Weasel gave him a dirty look. "In that closet there," he finally announced.

Ned took a shower. When he came out, Weasel and El Borracho were gone. In their place was a twelve- or thirteen-year-old boy who was playing some kind of card game with Speedy. He looked at Ned and said: "Wow, he really is white—looks like the principal from my school, only stupider."

"Thanks," Ned said in Spanish. "What do you have for me?"

"Over there, Mr. President," Speedy pointed at a knapsack by the fake fireplace under the TV and laughed. The boy, fat and suspicious-looking, joined him.

Ned walked over and picked it up. He put it on Speedy's dining room table and opened it up. The first thing that popped out was a Springfield M1911A1, a handgun Ned recognized and appreciated a great deal. It came with a couple of boxes of ammo. Deeper inside the pack was a Ziploc bag with about a half-gram of weed, a plastic grocery store shopping bag with about $15,000 in well-worn cash, and a "Support Your Local Cossacks" T-shirt.

"Weasel says for you to go shopping, buy some clothes," the boy said.

"I think I'll do that, little man," Ned answered.

Speedy spoke to the kid. "Run along now and do your kid things," he said. "We have man things to discuss."

As soon as he was sure the boy had left, Speedy looked angrily at Ned. "Don't get too comfortable," he said. "I know things about you."

Ned, trying to play it tough, picked up his gun. "Yeah, what do you know?"

"Things," he said. "Things you would rather I didn't know."

"You don't know shit," Ned said. "Because there is nothing to know. You're just pissed off because I'm president and you're just some low-level tough guy. Your job is to look after me, so look after me."

"Yeah, I'll do that," Speedy seethed. "Just sleep well."

"I will."

Chapter Eight

Ned had not taken Speedy's threats very seriously. He knew that Poco Loco was big time—he even had ambitions of ruling all of Mexico one day. And since Ned appeared to be a big part of his plans (at least to help establish and maintain a major revenue stream from Arizona), it would be a bad move, potentially a suicidal one, for the Cossacks to let anything happen to him. He knew intellectually and instinctively that Speedy wouldn't harm him while he was under his roof, but he slept with a loaded gun anyway.

When he woke up, he went into the living room and sat down. Speedy either wasn't awake yet or had left. Ned was hungry so he checked the fridge. He realized that he missed having the ranch-house girls taking care of him. All he could find in the fridge was old fast food that Speedy was keeping for some reason, but he was so hungry, he had little choice. If Speedy made a fuss, he'd just give him a hundred bucks or so to shut him up.

While Ned had his head in the fridge, the doorbell rang. Startled, he picked up his gun from the kitchen counter and approached the door. He peeked through the side window to see Weasel and another man on the stoop. The other guy was older, fatter, and had none of the affectations of a biker. In fact, he was wearing a blazer and slacks despite the already searing south Arizona sun. Ned let them in.

Weasel introduced the other guy as Carlos Garcia, and Ned shook his hand. Garcia smiled with the polish of a lifelong salesman, exposing a gold tooth with a diamond inlay. "It is a pleasure to meet you," he said. "I look forward to doing business with you."

"Business? That's great," Ned said. "What are we doing?"

Weasel explained that Garcia owned a small chain of bars and fast-food outlets along Interstate 19 from Catalina, a suburb north of Tucson, all the way down to a few hundred yards from the border in Nogales. Ribs, chicken wings, and fries places, they targeted a non-Hispanic clientele and were moderately successful. The real money came in augmenting his revenue with drug sales. "But right now," Weasel said. "We're finding it very hard to sell anything stronger than weed. The cowboys and other white trash around here just don't trust the Mexicans. We need one of you guys to win them over."

"So I'll be selling?"

"No," Garcia assured him. "All you have to do is show up, be visible; interact with the guys who are actually selling. Try to make them look like they're your friends, like they're trustworthy. Hang out, pat them on the back, play pool with them, or whatever."

"That's all?"

"Well, if you can make friends with any of the locals, that's even better—especially if they're connected," said Garcia. "And if you can make any deals on your own, that's gravy."

"What about the cops?"

"The cops aren't a problem unless you do something wrong—they only come in to my places to look for illegals in the kitchen," Garcia said. "Everything's in my name. You're not officially on staff, just a noteworthy and popular customer. They won't even see you because they're just not looking for you."

"Any bad guys?"

Garcia paused. "A little while ago, I would have warned you about the Hells Angels, but they are done around here now."

"So what are we waiting for?" asked Ned.

* * *

Tovar and Weise wasted no time once they arrived in Arizona. Weise's enthusiasm was obvious, and Tovar liked not just the company but the feeling that they were getting something done. There was nowhere in Sahuarita for them to stay, so they were located in Green Valley, just south of Tucson. It was nine a.m. local time when they arrived at the lab. What remained of the bike was twisted and charred. The motorcycle expert they had called in from Flagstaff had finished his examination and determined that it was, in all likelihood, the same bike that had been registered to Eric Steadman in Delaware.

The local police had interviewed Lucas's friends, family, and business associates, focusing on the bike. Those who knew of the motorcycle pointed out that Lucas could not stop boasting about it after it had arrived. According to his brother-in-law, Caleb McInytre, Lucas claimed that he was given the bike in payment from a supplier who was facing bankruptcy. When he was pressed on who, Lucas only told him it was someone from back east, someone McIntyre didn't know.

Tovar called McIntyre in. They questioned him about Lucas and his business associates, then asked him if he had seen Aiken, handing him some photos they had from when he was in the witness-protection program. McIntyre said he hadn't seen anyone like that around Sahuarita, but he'd be sure to get back to them if he did. Despite that one particular dead end, the two agents agreed that they were getting closer to Aiken. If was in the area, they thought, it wouldn't be too long before they found him.

* * *

Weasel and Garcia directed Ned to a black Infiniti sedan. Weasel instructed Ned to sit up front, so he could give him a guided tour. They drove south to Nogales, to show Ned the first of the places he would be hanging out in on their behalf.

There wasn't much to this particular Gibby's Bar-B-Q location—just a storefront with melamine tables and chairs and a counter behind which a Mexican staff prepared and served various fast-food versions of classic barbecue favorites. Melendez introduced Ned to them as Colin, the new manager. The employees greeted him and were surprised at how well he spoke Spanish.

They took him to a strip mall farther north in town. At one end of the mall was a bar called Good Time Dave's. Again, it was a pretty basic place—some stools at a bar, a pool table, and a smattering of cowboy-related memorabilia. The few men drinking in there barely acknowledged the trio when they entered. Again Garcia introduced Ned as Colin, the new manager.

Back in the car, Ned asked Weasel what happened to the old manager.

"He was stupid," answered the big man, who refused to elaborate further.

They toured a number of Gibby's and Dave's locations, each with the same result. The staff greeted him politely, if not warmly, while the customers barely seemed to notice his presence. At the last Gibby's stop in Catalina, Garcia told the staff to pack up some ribs, chicken, and fries for Weasel and Ned to bring to the Cossacks' club house.

They left Garcia there, and drove to the Barrio El Hoyo neighborhood on the east side of Tucson. They pulled up in front of a store called XXX-Caliber Guns & Ammo. Although the building was only about thirty feet wide, it was at least eighty feet long. "We normally go around back, but I want to introduce you to Scruffy," Weasel told Ned, who was carrying enough Gibby's barbecue to feed a college class. "You'll like this."

As they entered the gun shop, Weasel was immediately approached by an ancient man in an old-style wheelchair, the kind in which the rider moves the chair with his hands on the wheels. He was small and frail and looked like he hadn't seen the sun in years. His bald head reflected the overhead lights and his stringy beard made it almost down to his lap. "How ya doin' there, Weezie?" he shouted through his three remaining teeth as he rolled over to Weasel. "Didja bring some Gibby's? Didja?"

"Yeah, yeah, Scruffy, I got you some chicken," Weasel said as he handed a white cardboard box of chicken and fries—the grease already turning it transparent in spots—to Scruffy. "And Scruffy, this is Ian or Colin or Crash or something—the new white guy."

Scruffy cackled wildly while diving into the box of chicken pieces and French fries. "I thought I was your favorite white guy!"

Weasel laughed warmly. "Yeah, you are Scruffy," he said. "But you're retired, man, you're an institution. We need this guy to be the face of the franchise—you know, window dressing."

But it didn't matter what he said. Scruffy was so deep into his chicken that he couldn't hear him anyway. Weasel then turned and faced the display case. Behind it was an immense man, at least 400 pounds, and definitely bigger than El Ratón. The huge man had a beard down to his belt buckle and tattoos covering his neck and arms. He had a scar on his face that ran from the center of his forehead over his left eye and down his left cheek.

"This is the new guy, Stew Bob," Weasel said to him. "Just call him Colin."

"Colin? I ain't gonna call this one shit," Stew Bob snorted while retrieving enough phlegm to make a dramatic spit. "He ain't gonna last. I can always tell." Then he laughed, staring into Ned's eyes the whole time.

"Whatever, Stew Bob," Weasel said, and rolled his eyes. "C'mon, Crash, through here." The big biker led him through a back door about twenty feet beyond the door they entered the building from. It was marked "Employees Only: Trespassers will be shot and pissed on."

Ned's eyes took a moment to adjust to the light beyond the door. Inside, he saw an office not unlike those of the accountants he and his fellow members of the Sons of Satan had mocked when he was a new recruit to the biker lifestyle. "This is where we keep track of every transaction," Weasel told him. "People will tell you that I only do it to make the Clown happy, but I would do it anyway. It just makes financial and disciplinary sense—can't have the men stealing or holding out, can we?"

"Definitely not."

They passed through the office without stopping and entered a large luxurious room. There was a bar and a dance floor and couches angled to encourage conversation. "This is it, hope you like it," said Weasel. "You were what— Lawbreakers? Bandidos?"

"Sons."

"Really? Oh, well, you're gonna find us a lot more on the ball than what you're used to," Weasel said.

"We like to have fun, but business has to come first. You know."

"Yeah, I know," Ned said. "You know where I've been for the last few months."

Weasel laughed derisively. "I don't mean to offend you, man, but those are Mexicans, we are Mexican-Americans," he said. "There's a big difference. You won't find us selling oranges by the freeway or hanging bodies from the overpass; we are all business. We're here to get rich,"

"Or die tryin'?"

"Yeah," he chuckled. "Or die tryin', just like everyone who comes to America. Can I get you a drink?"

"I thought you were all business?"

"This is our business," Weasel said. "Well, sort of. We don't deal booze because booze is legal, so there is no money in it. We do sell weed—which you may indulge in, in moderation—but prefer to move coke, meth, and heroin. But using any of those will get you a death sentence, and not from an overdose, you understand?"

Ned, though nervous, did his best not to betray his feelings. "That's the universal rule," he said. "I have been around, you know."

"Yeah, from what I've heard, you've been everywhere," Weasel said. "But somehow you still come off as an innocent, a real Herbie, like some guy who . . . who . . . I dunno, some guy who's gonna sell me insurance or foreclose on my mortgage or something."

Ned just smiled.

"I guess that's why they want you," Weasel said in a friendlier tone than Ned had heard in years. "You're like that guy who does the cartoon voices, man, you have a gift."

Ned smiled again. "Ah, man, I could sell ice to the Eskimos, sand to the Arabs. . ."

". . . and beans to the Mexicans, right?"

Ned felt a moment of uneasiness, but could scan no malevolence in Weasel's face. "You want beans, man?" he said in his best imitation of a carnival huckster. "I got beans that will blow your mind."

Weasel laughed. "Just spread those ribs out on the table, man," he said. "I'll grab some brews and we can talk business. But first I have to take your picture."

* * *

After the intern had spent the entire trip learning about the ways of the FBI from the veteran, Tovar and Weise started discussing the case in earnest over lunch at a Chik-Fil-A on the west side of Tucson. "While it is true the bike could have changed hands a few times, it's unlikely," Tovar said. "Something as noticeable as that causes people to talk, especially in small towns."

"Yeah, and the timing works out perfectly," Weise agreed. "If Aiken rode the bike all the way from New York City, he would have arrived at about the same time Lucas acquired it. But why Lucas? Why here?"

"I have a theory related to both those questions, but I'm not sure they jibe with each other," Tovar said.

"What stands out about Lucas to me is that he's in the air-conditioning business, and Aiken worked for an air-conditioning company in Delaware. My research tells me that Hawkridge and Lucas's company are direct competitors and that there is no love lost between Andersson—Aiken's old boss—and Lucas, but it's too much of a connection not to explore."

"And the place?"

"There's not really a whole lot here for a Midwestern biker on the run from the Sons and the FBI," he said. "If he was still a member in good standing with the club, any club, I would conjecture that he's here to take advantage of the drug-dealing vacuum created by the arrests of all those Hells Angels."

"But no crew would want a snitch, especially an FBI informant," Weise said. "Is it possible that he could be using an assumed identity?"

"What, another one?" Tovar laughed. "I'm not sure this guy can handle the two he already has." Then he turned serious. "These bikers, I know them," he said. "They may not be all that smart, but they are pretty crafty. And they are absolutely paranoid when it comes to informants . . . there's no way they wouldn't figure out who he was after a while and that would really, really suck for him."

Weise smiled. "And the other option, of course, is about an hour's drive south of us."

"Maybe a few years ago," Tovar said. "But Mexico, especially the northern part, is in an all-out war at this point. He'd be safer with the bikers than he would with those people."

"Yeah, I know that and you know that," Weise pointed out. "But does he know that?"

"If he didn't, then this line of inquiry is at an end," Tovar said. "If he went down there, his body is probably in a dumpster or chopped up for dog food by now—those guys don't mess around."

* * *

Back in the clubhouse, Weasel explained how the Cossacks work. "It's just like most clubs—you have to have a bike, respect for the patch, and all that," he said. "We're not fanatics about it like the Hells Angels or the Sons of Satan, but we do respect it."

"Understood."

"Because of your position, you won't have to wear the patch very often; just on special occasions like funerals and stuff," he continued. "But you have to have a Harley-Davidson, it's in the bylaws. We can get one to you when we find you a place to live. Don't worry about license, insurance, and all that—we have people."

"What about cops?"

"Mostly untouchable around here, bunch of Dudley Do-Rights, but we have a fixer at central processing who can take care of minor shit," Weasel said with apparent pride. "Best rule of thumb for you would be to avoid getting into trouble in the first place—your role is as a talker, so don't carry any shit on you at all, ever, stay out of fights, drive the speed limit, don't drink and drive, and stay away from women who could be trouble."

"And if I do get arrested?"

"We don't know each other," Weasel said with some gravity. "That's why you are forbidden to get a Cossacks tattoo. See, unlike the Hells and the Sons, we sell our logo to anyone who wants it. If you go down and they find any Cossacks stuff in your shit, then all we have to say is that you're just another wannabe. If they find a phone with my number in it, I'll say you're stalking me because you want to join and I won't let you, got it?"

"Got it."

"We'll have you set up by tomorrow night," Weasel's tone turned warmer. "Nice place, used to be a store, but it's fixed up pretty trendy. You're from back east, you'll love it."

"And the bike?"

"Well, the bylaw says you have to have a Harley, but they don't say that it has to be new or all that good," he said. "There's a 1999 Sportster we can have for you. It's nothing special—traditional 883 engine, pure stock, black paint, nothing added other than one of those little plastic windshields."

"Sounds fine." Ned was beginning to think that the little bike could have potential if he was going to stay in the area for any length of time. "Stolen? Should I be worried?"

"Quite the opposite. It will be all legal under your name, but it's for you to own, not ride—except on the same occasions where you'd wear a patch," Weasel instructed. "Mostly, you'll be driving. Since you're supposed be a relatively successful bar and fast-food manager, you have to have a pretty nice ride—it's a Jaguar X-Type, a 2006 I think.

Rare for these parts, but doesn't really get much attention from the doughnut gang."

"Not bad at all," Ned said, with memories of his Kia, his Tempo, and his Subaru quickly fading.

The pair ran through the details of the job a couple more times until Weasel was satisfied Ned knew exactly what was expected of him. Then he showed him the back-room with a cot where Ned was expected to sleep the night and where he would shower in the morning.

Back in the clubhouse's main room, the two talked about the differences between Arizona, the Midwest, and the East Coast, and Weasel told Ned about some of the characters he'd meet on the Tucson streets. He told him that Scruffy, despite his appearance, was always to be treated well, and that Stew Bob was all talk and not a threat. They talked into the night until Weasel said he had to get back to his wife and kids. Before he left, he asked Ned for all of his identification. Ned handed him Ian Wuerth's wallet. "No, not that," he said. "Your real stuff." Ned gave him the Eric Steadman identification that the FBI had given him. "That's better," Weasel said.

Ned slept fitfully that night on the cot, wondering if Gibby and Stew Bob were still in the building with him and if the Cossacks were smart enough to figure out who he really was.

* * *

Part of Tovar's job in Tuscon was to liaise with local law enforcement. According to them, the area had long been a transit point for drugs moving elsewhere in the western United States and Canada, most of them being distributed through crime organizations in Denver, which acted as a regional hub for all kinds of gangs from the Salvadoran MS-13, the Los Angeles–based Crips, and the Sicilian Cosa Nostra. Even the Russians, Chinese, and Vietnamese had major operations there.

Tovar and Weise later agreed that law enforcement in southeastern Arizona were stretched to their financial, personnel, and constitutional limits, and that they were more than happy to see that the big players were someone else's problem.

They warned the two FBI officers about entering Mexico, but said that there was little violence in their own area, despite the all-out war just on the other side. As far as local trafficking was concerned, it had long been in the hands of the Hells Angels, but since the ATF had severely crippled them, their network had fallen apart.

When Tovar asked who was dealing on the streets, the top gangs officer, Detective Frank Ojeda, shrugged. "It's a hodgepodge right now, it's almost like there's a vacuum," he said. "It makes me think someone is going to come in and reap the benefits of the Hells Angels' old infrastructure and contacts."

"So there are no existing gangs in the area?"

"Yeah, but they are all Mexican," said Ojeda. "And that limits who they can sell to around here."

"What about bikers?" Weise asked. "Other than the Hells Angels."

"We have one chapter of the Cossacks," Ojeda said. "But they're all Mexican too, so they generally just sell to other Mexicans—small time, to be sure, but worth keeping an eye on. I think they help transport significant amounts north, especially now the Hells Angels are out of the way."

"So you're kind of waiting this out," Tovar asked. "Seeing who pounces? Like the Bandidos or Vagos or whoever?"

"Kind of," Ojeda told him. "You want to know more? Just talk to Rasmussen over at the ATF."

* * *

When Weasel, Speedy, and two other Mexican-looking bikers showed up the following afternoon, Ned had been waiting nervously, pecking at leftover barbecue. He'd watched the news on TV all day and was fascinated by the fact that a mass grave had been found in Mexico. It wasn't in Sonora, so it was unlikely that anyone he knew was involved, but it was Mexico, and it was people in his business. According to CNN, an informant had told the military that he and another man had disposed of some bodies in an old silver mine shaft in the state of Durango, which Ned knew was deep in the Sinaloa Cartel's territory. The authorities went down the shaft to recover the bodies, but they found out that they were on top of other bodies, which were on top of even more bodies. By noon, they had recovered thirty-five. By the time the Cossacks showed up a little after two, the number had grown to seventy-one, but they couldn't be sure because some were just parts.

Speedy saw what Ned was watching. "Those your guys?" he asked.

It took Ned a moment to realize what was going on. "Uh, no, no, that was way down in Durango," he said.

"Hmmm, looks like the work of the Zetas," said Weasel. "Not only is it their way of doing business, but Durango is in the Sinaloa Cartel's backyard—body dumps are always on your enemy's turf."

"Zetas?"

"Jeez, man, I thought you were the guy who was down there," said Weasel derisively. "Los Zetas, c'mon man, they were a bunch of soldiers who received special training— y'know, like urban warfare and all that—from you guys and the Israelis and the Brits."

"And they fight the cartels?"

"They did, but not for long. The Gulf Cartel offered them more money and they switched sides. They used to work for the Gulf Cartel against the other cartels," Weasel said. "Until they got bigger than the Gulf Cartel and now they are their own cartel who fights everyone."

"What?"

Weasel sighed. "I can't believe you don't know this: your people trained the Zetas, then told them to go back to their $200-a-week jobs in the army and the cartels offer them more than $1,000 a week for the same work," he said. "You'd make the same choice, just like La Linea up in Juarez and a whole bunch of others in other places. It's *plata o plomo.*"

"*Plata o plomo*?"

"Yeah, silver or lead, man," Weasel smiled. "Silver as in getting paid or lead as in a bullet to the brain—you work with us and be rewarded, or you work against us and die. It's not a difficult choice for most people."

"Makes sense," said Ned. "We have bad cops, too."

Speedy looked intensely offended. "No, no, no, you don't understand. Here you have a hundred cops—one takes bribes, one breaks heads because he enjoys it, but the other ninety-eight do their jobs more or less cleanly," he said. "But in Mexico, of one hundred cops, one hundred take bribes and one hundred bust heads. Everyone is on the take—mayors, governors. I wouldn't even be surprised if Calderón himself gets a paper bag from El Chapo every week."

Obviously trying to change the subject, Weasel indicated the report on TV. "Up to seventy-one?" he said. "That's just one short of the record."

"But those were whole bodies, not just parts," said one of the guys Ned didn't know. "The body count on the farm in Tamaulipas was up around a hundred before they started putting all the parts together . . . then it fell to seventy-two."

"He's right," said Speedy. "Once they start putting them together like Lego, the count starts to fall. I give this one maybe fifty-four, fifty-five."

"Body counts? The farm?" Ned asked. "What are you guys talking about?"

One of the guys Ned didn't know laughed. "It's funny, I'd say ironic if I was sure I knew exactly what that meant," he said. "You were living in Mexico and had no idea what was going on down there and we're up here—safe from all the lunacy—and we know everything."

Weasel gave him a serious look. "He didn't know because they don't report that shit down there," he said. "If they do, they kill the reporter."

Speedy laughed. "Kind of makes you appreciate how lucky we Americans have it," he said, looking at Ned. "And how bad those Mexicans have it."

"So this sort of thing happens all the time?" Ned asked, incredulous.

"Yep, get used to it, man," Weasel said. "You're in America now, so you can learn the truth about Mexico—you know that more than 50,000 people have been murdered in the Mexican drug war in less than five years? Don't say yes, because I know you didn't. You would never have gone down there if you did."

"So why don't they kill the American reporters?"

"Some of the guys down there, they keep their organizations together and motivated by telling them that they are 'freedom fighters' working to bring down the oppressive government—they think the American reporters will help their cause," said Weasel. "But it's all a scam, they're just drug dealers; but they have to keep the illusion alive for a steady stream of new recruits."

"So do you get that kind of violence here?"

"Nope, stops at the border," said Weasel. "The cartel guys might be deluded, but they're not stupid—that's a fight they'd rather not pick."

"Sometimes a dealer will get popped for not paying his debts," said Speedy. "Or for cooperating with the Federales."

"But that's rare," said Weasel. "Generally the cartels just want to sell up here. Any violence would just get in the way of that. It's all about the Benjamins."

Ned knew he looked relieved and he had that feeling of delayed panic one feels after realizing the danger they had previously been in. "Let's get us some," he said in a tone he hoped would be interpreted as enthusiastic. "When do I start?"

"That's what I like to hear," said Weasel. "We're actually here to take you to your new place—the Sportster and the Jaguar should be there already."

"New ID?"

"Yeah, remember the pictures I took last night?" he said. "I had our guy insert them into a driver's license, passport, and a couple of other cards—should be done today."

"How good are they?"

"Perfect, they're real." Weasel looked a touch offended. "Just the picture's changed. I wouldn't use the passport at an airport, though."

"Real?"

"Yeah," said Speedy. "We know a guy who had an 'unfortunate accident' and they never found his body."

"Came from back east, didn't have a family, didn't have any friends other than us, so nobody is asking any questions," Weasel added. "You are kind of taking over his place. Everything works, from his credit cards—you may want to call them and tell them you forgot your PIN—to his license and registration, even his life insurance."

They discussed more of the logistics of Ned's new job before piling into Weasel's giant Chevy Tahoe SUV.

They drove through downtown Tucson to an old store on North Meyer Avenue. The giant windows up front that had previously shown small appliances and electronics were now blinded by southwestern-motif drapes. Inside it was decorated fairly well. It suited the life of a single man with some money and few responsibilities. Ned thought it could be quite pleasant once he added some of his own things.

Weasel showed him around. In the bedroom, he produced a key ring from his pocket and unlocked a gun locker under the bed. Inside were two handguns and two rifles. "These are registered to you, so be careful,"

Back in the living room, Speedy and the guy whose name Ned didn't know were sitting down. "Aren't you gonna offer us a beer?" Speedy asked.

"Yeah, I guess so," Ned answered. "I'll see what's in the fridge."

"He's just joking, man, said Weasel. "We gotta go— don't you go anywhere until the kid gets here, Seriously. You get stopped by a cop and you're done, man." He left the key ring he used to open the gun locker on Ned's coffee table.

They left, and Ned waited. Despite the oppressive heat, he waited outside. After about an hour, a Mexican-looking kid rode by on a bike. He circled the block and came around again. He stopped in front of the store. "You the guy?' he asked Ned.

"I guess so."

"You better be the guy."

"I am."

"Here," the kid said and handed Ned a large envelope.

Ned handed the kid a twenty, then went back inside. He poured the contents of the envelope onto his coffee table. It was a wallet and a passport. He opened up the passport and saw himself looking back. "Okay, so I'm Colin McCarthy."

* * *

The ATF officers were exactly as Tovar had feared—all steroided-up musclemen with shaved heads, goatees, and wraparound sunglasses who spoke too loudly. The FBI agents were led to Detective Rasmussen's office on the fourth floor of what appeared to them like a fortress, even by FBI standards.

Rasmussen was friendly, but tight-lipped. After a great deal of negotiation, Tovar convinced him to let the FBI in on their current operation involving motorcycle gangs in the area because of the likelihood that Aiken would seek out any bikers if he was in the area. "We're trying to repeat the success we had when Jaybird Dobyns infiltrated the Hells Angels," Rasmussen said. "We have some men who are posing as an outlaw biker gang moving in from Colorado."

Tovar was dumbfounded. He was sure the same plan would not work twice and it showed great hubris on the ATF's part to try it again. "Who are they infiltrating?"

"That's the beauty of it," Rasmussen said. "This new gang—the Tortured Souls—will set up just south of Tucson and let it be known they are open for business. Then when someone comes in to challenge them, we get our evidence."

"So you're setting up a trap, and hoping someone walks into it?"

"You might say that, but only because you're not from down here," Rasmussen said bluntly. "The Mexicans are overrunning the area with drugs carried in on illegals. These people near the border have had enough, they are scared for their lives, and there's no way we can stop the violence from spilling over the border if they think they can get away with it. Make no mistake—drugs will be sold in southeastern Arizona, and we want to catch the organizers whether they are here already or not."

"So when is all this happening?"

"Already started, the Souls have bought a house just outside Sahuarita and are setting it up as a clubhouse," Rasmussen sounded proud. "They have colors, tats, bikes, guns, the whole bit. I used to be a street cop and detective up in Wisconsin and I can tell you these guys really look the part. Just like the Outlaws I used to deal with."

"Well, there is a strong chance that if our man Aiken is in the area, he will try to get into contact with your men," Tovar said. "He may even try to join them."

"In that event, I will let you know immediately."

Chapter Nine

It was hot, it was dry, and it was boring—but Ned loved it. Being back in the relative safety of the United States—a place he understood, no matter how far off the mainstream he got—was something he never realized how much he appreciated before. There were all kinds of people out for his head in the States, but it was something he could deal with, something he understood. He felt secure, despite the obvious threats, because he knew that Poco Loco had his back. Not like Mexico, where violence and death just seems to come out of the blue.

Ned walked out of his luxurious home to his Jaguar, got in and turned the key. The hum of the engine was joined by the welcome blast of the air conditioner. He turned on the stereo and was disappointed that all the preset stations were classic rock or country. He hit scan over and over again until he found something a little more modern. He finally came across an old Eminem song. It wasn't perfect, but it was good enough.

He drove down Highway 19 to Nogales. He stopped in the southernmost Gibby's location within sight of the border. He greeted the staff, who nodded politely and asked him what he wanted. Breakfast choices at a fast-food barbecue restaurant are limited, so he decided on the breakfast burrito—powdered scrambled eggs with bits of chorizo and processed cheese wrapped in a sodium-laden wheat tortilla. After his first bite, he longed for the girls at the ranch house and their exquisite cooking.

Nobody took much notice of him until a couple of tough-looking guys came to sit with him. "You're Crash?" one asked.

"Yeah."

"I'm Chancho," the guy said. "We're supposed to help each other."

"I understand."

"So how do you want to do this?"

"Well, we're supposed to be seen together," Ned told him. "Supposed to hang out, so let's just hang out."

"Uhh, okay," Chancho said. "How do we do that?"

"Just start talking."

And Chancho did just that, joined by his partner, Little Willie. They spoke about their cars first, and told tales of bad drivers and accidents they almost had. From there it went to sports, about how the Cardinals' recent Super Bowl run was just a mirage—all quarterback Kurt Warner's doing, and now that he was retired, they looked like they'd never be close to being a winning team ever again.

All in all, it was a fairly pleasant way to spend a half-hour. The dealers turned out to be pretty interesting guys. After finishing his breakfast with Chancho and Little Willie, Ned drove up to the next spot on his route, another Gibby's about three miles up Highway 19. Because he had already had breakfast at the first one, he just ordered coffee. He was soon approached by another dealer—this one named Fermino—who sat with him. After an awkward few minutes, Ned encouraged him to talk about his motorcycle. Although Ned had never really had a great deal of interest in Japanese sports bikes, he knew enough to keep Fermino comfortable and keep up his end of the conversation.

The process repeated itself until he had visited the last Gibby's. After taking a break at Balboa Heights Park, Ned started visiting every Dave's location in the area. It was a little harder to talk in the bars, which could be loud with music and shouting, but he met his connections at each one and started talking. The hardest part was being in bars in such a hot climate and not being able to drink any beer. But Ned knew that a drinking and driving arrest could put him behind bars forever, so he laid off the alcohol until he got home.

That first day, Ned actually visited all fifteen of Garcia's franchises. It was a remarkable amount of driving and the process took him well into the night. To save driving time and allow himself more face time at each outlet, Ned decided he would hit three a day, visiting each location once a week, taking Sundays and Mondays off. He'd rotate them, so that he didn't spend every Tuesday night in the same bar or every Saturday morning at the same rib joint. Of course, adjustments could be made if it meant a potential deal.

The dealers were all kind of the same—Mexican-American men in their early twenties who had a look of street toughness that Ned understood made many people nervous. His job as a gateway between them and potential customers became quickly apparent.

But he had been visiting the bars and rib joints for two weeks without any action, He saw Melendez once, but they didn't acknowledge each other. He also ran into Weasel, who assured him everything was cool, despite the fact he hadn't seen any action yet, and that things would pick up. The drug drought created in the community by the downfall of the Hells Angels would force people to come to Ned.

And a day later, someone did. Ned was sitting in a Gibby's, nursing a coffee and reading the *Tucson Citizen,* waiting for his contact when a woman took the seat across from him. She was a little older than him, her hair was dyed blonde, and she seemed ordinary in just about every way. She introduced herself as Marni. At first, she was slightly flirtatious, but gave that up when she saw Ned wasn't biting. After some small talk about the quality of Gibby's food— they agreed it was just a step or two above atrocious—she revealed her true intentions. "My husband and I are having a party, and we'd like you to come," she said.

"Whoa, what kind of party?" From the look in her eye, Ned knew what she was talking about, but wanted to force her to be more direct. "I don't know . . ."

"Nothing like that, silly," she said. "Just a get-together with some friends and coworkers to blow off some steam. It's been crazy around here for the past few weeks, months even."

"But why me?"

"Well, I've been watching you," Marni said conspiratorially. "You're new here, you seem nice, you dress very well, and you don't seem to have any friends."

"I have friends," Ned corrected her. "I was waiting for one when we met."

"Oh yes, the Mexican fellow," she acknowledged. "Seems a bit rough." It sounded like a question.

"Not really, he just dresses that way," and then he lowered the boom. "It's the business he's in."

Marni smiled and nodded. "I'd invite him, too, but it wouldn't look right, you know."

"I understand completely," Ned said. "But I think I'm just a bit too busy to go to a party right now. How about if I just send a little something along in my place?"

Marni sighed and smiled. "That would be perfect!" she said. "As long as we are talking about the right 'little something' at the right price."

At that moment, Ned's contact, Chancho walked in. Seeing Ned talking to someone else, Chancho ordered some food and sat at a different table.

Ned nodded at Marni, then at Chancho. "It's very, very good and it is, from what I hear, the only game in town, so the price is the price," he told her. "I'm sure you'll be satisfied with it."

"So how do we do this?" she asked.

"Well, I don't handle anything myself, so let me introduce you to my friend Chancho," Ned said, indicating Chancho, who was staring at his food and looked up only after hearing his name.

Marni's eyes betrayed her tension. "Oh, I couldn't," she said. "Can't I just deal with you?"

"I'm sorry, but it's like I said, I don't handle anything, ever," Ned told her and gestured for Chancho to come over. He did, and brought his food with him. "Marnie, this is Chancho—don't let his looks deceive you, he's just a regular guy, even has a pet hamster."

"It's not mine, it's my daughter's," Chancho said sheepishly. Marni smiled. Ned continued to engage both in conversation, and when he felt Marni was confident enough to make a deal with Chancho, he left them to it.

It was the first of what became a small flood of customers. Ned had met more people who approached him as Marni had, and many of them sent friends. After two more weeks of making his rounds, Ned had hooked up at least one customer in each location and a total of seven different clients at one particularly meth-hungry Dave's location.

As the number of clients ballooned, Ned's role finally made sense to him. The users were there all along, and so were the dealers, but the two groups were separated by too many cultural divides for either to make the crucial first move. Without him, drugs didn't get sold; with him, they did.

The Cossacks needed him, Poco Loco needed him. He was the key to their whole business.

The days settled into a pleasant routine. Ned would wake up early—it was the first time in years that he could sleep well enough to do so—before the sun had burned off the nighttime coolness, and went for a run. He got to know several other morning joggers and they would often trade jokes or just talk. Then he'd shower, fire up the Jaguar, and head off to his first visit of the day. He didn't really like the breakfast they served at Gibby's, so he had gotten the cooks just to scramble him some real eggs and serve it with sausage and a biscuit. Then he'd go to his next location for lunch and to another for dinner.

When he went to a Dave's, he always had someone to talk with or a game to play, but at Gibby's, he tended to read the newspaper, buying both the *Citizen* and the *Arizona Daily Star*. He immediately went to the Mexico section of each paper, as he had become fascinated by the news from down there. While in Mexico, he knew it was rough and violent, that the cartels and the government were fighting each other, but he had no idea of the scope of things. It was hard to tell from the hit-and-miss reporting of the American papers, but it seemed to Ned that literally thousands, maybe tens of thousands of people were being murdered every year. And it wasn't just the number of murders that stunned him. There were slaughters—forty people here, fifty there—people killed for the most mundane of reasons. Bodies were displayed in public places. Body parts were sent to police or the families of the victims. Crowds of innocent people were targeted simply to scare an opposing cartel by nothing more than its pure coldhearted brutality. It was as though the whole country had gone crazy. He knew he had developed more than a passing interest when he found a store that sold the *New York Times* and started buying it for its Mexico coverage, looking especially for mention of the Jalisco Cartel or Poco Loco himself.

* * *

To an outside observer, it didn't look as though the ATF had picked the right man for the job. Wayne "Big Red" Hauser was tall, but unlike most southwestern bikers, he was not overly muscled or covered in tattoos. Instead of the shaved head, multiple piercings, and thick beards most of his type had, Hauser looked like he could be in just about any business. He was handsome, but not remarkably so, and had the commanding presence of a future CEO. Rather than arouse suspicion by sending in an obvious stereotype of a long-haired, big-bellied biker, the ATF craftily recruited a more modern style of outlaw biker, the gangster businessman. Before he was an agent, Hauser was in the navy. He had failed his test to become a SEAL because of a lack of focus, and left the service.

He rode his ancient Harley—its thundering pipes shattering the calm wherever he took it—through the streets of Tucson from his home to the clubhouse he and some fellow officers had set up. He even had a fellow officer posing as his wife. She agreed to be tattooed, but maintained her own bedroom.

Big Red and eight other agents made up the Tortured Souls. Their cover story—which the ATF had leaked to local media, law enforcement, and their informant community— was that they were an independent Denver-based gang with three chapters in Colorado, and their government-made website backed it up. Said to be aligned with, but not actually that close to the Outlaws, the Tortured Souls were supposed to be making a push into Arizona to take advantage of the weakened Hells Angels. The members all looked like bikers, wore leather jackets with their patch—a skull surrounded by flames—and rode Harleys. To help underscore their claims of authenticity, Big Red was said to have beaten the rap after having murdered a Hells Angel in Salt Lake City.

Like Ned, Big Red and his men did little more than be seen on the streets of Tucson, Nogales, and all the towns in between. But unlike Ned, they did their best to let people know exactly who they were—or at least who they were pretending to be. The Tortured Souls would frequent bars in the area and almost invariably cause trouble. At one, a strip joint called The Cap'n's Booty, they picked a fight with some tough-looking guys inside, causing more than $100,000 in damage. Big Red was arrested for aggravated assault, but was released when the arresting officers found out that he was an ATF agent. After that, Big Red embraced his character and did whatever he wanted when he wanted, protected from prosecution by his status as an agent and from retribution by his size and malevolence. His superiors at the ATF frowned on that kind of behavior, but considered the mission too important and Big Red too essential to its success to pull him from it.

At the clubhouse, he asked Nickels, one of his fellow Tortured Souls, about what he had learned after a week on the street. "People are freaking out over how dry the streets are since the Hells Angels went down," he told him. "The Mexicans have some shit, but nothing big time."

"That's it?" Big Red asked. "What about the other biker gang, the Cossacks?"

"All Mexican," Nickels replied. "And down here, it seems like Mexicans just sell to Mexicans."

"That'll change," Big Red said. "When people want drugs, they'll find a way to get them. And they always want drugs."

"So you think the Cossacks are going to be the big target?"

"Unless someone else comes in," he said. "Let's keep an eye on them. It's only a matter of time before people start knocking on their door." Big Red thought to himself that he'd go out and find someone himself if he had to.

*   *   *

It wasn't easy, but Tovar managed to convince Meloni to allow him and Weise to stay in Tucson a few more days. Meloni had wanted to pull them once he found out that the ATF was running its own sting operation that overlapped with the Aiken investigation, but Tovar argued that if Aiken were indeed in the area, he was unlikely to seek out an outlaw biker gang, new or not. And he pointed out that if the

ATF solved the Kuzik case it would look bad not just on them, but on the FBI itself.

They distributed pictures of him, claiming he was a missing person who required his medication. They didn't expect a big response, but it was the kind of thing that showed they were still working the case in Arizona, that allowed them to keep investigating Lucas and his ties on both sides of the border.

They interviewed Bryan Latos, who had taken over Lucas's business on behalf of his family. He didn't know much about the bike, just that some bankrupt guy back east had given it to the boss. Latos had pressed Lucas on the provenance of the bike. It was his job to account for every penny the company spent and took in and that the bike, he found out from the Internet, could be worth upwards of $35,000. But Lucas wouldn't budge; he told Latos to take it out of his personal account. Latos didn't push further. It was Lucas's company and he did things his own, stubborn way. He told the agents he would love to give them more information, but just didn't have any.

When they asked him about Lucas's dealings in Mexico, Latos became visibly nervous. "We have a wholly owned subsidiary in Heroica Nogales—on the Mexican side—called Holsamex," he told them. "It assembles components, taking advantage of favorable labor costs."

"Any trouble down there?"

"What do you mean?"

"Well, there's a war going on in Mexico." Tovar said. "People are dying left, right, and center."

"Our shipments have not been interrupted."

Tovar rolled his eyes at Weise, who acknowledged the agent's exasperation with a laugh. They asked Latos if he knew Ned Aiken, Eric Steadman, or Mark Troutman. He didn't seem to know anything about Ned under either name, but correctly identified Troutman as an employee of Lucas's who had died.

* * *

Ned was making a scheduled stop at a Dave's when he noticed Weasel and El Borracho inside. They greeted him warmly and asked him to sit with them. "You have been a very busy man," Weasel said to Ned. "Very busy indeed."

Ned was confused. "Busy?"

"I'll say," said El Borracho. "Business is booming."

"Booming?"

"Yeah, thanks to you, we have all kinds of new revenue streams," Weasel said. "This idea from your friend down south of the border is absolute genius."

"He is a pretty smart guy," Ned said, assuming they were both talking about Poco Loco. "I'm just glad I can help."

"Well, let us help you," Weasel said. "Party, tonight, at the clubhouse. We'll have some real barbecue, not this fast-food shit."

Ned agreed, and after talking to a few other friends he had at that Dave's location, he left with the Cossacks.

The yard behind the clubhouse had been fixed up with lights, tables, and chairs. There was music—ranging from *narcocorridas* to ZZ Top—food, drinks, and guests. A number of the bikers friends, wives, and girlfriends had showed up, and a few of the girls from the Blue Moon Saloon—a strip joint that Speedy ran as a side business—were there as well. Scruffy appeared to be asleep in a shaded spot beside the doorway, but Stew Bob did not show.

It was a welcoming atmosphere, and Ned began to have a good time. He had a couple of beers (not enough to get drunk and sloppy) and spoke with some of the girls. At least he was having a good time until Speedy arrived, already quite drunk. "So there he is, the big hero," he said to Ned. "You think you're so hot just because you have friends south of the border. Well, I have friends down there, too, and they have been talking about you."

Ned stood and faced his accuser. "Oh yeah?" he asked. "And what do your friends have to say about me."

"Plenty!" he shouted. "That you're a coward, a fag, and maybe even an undercover agent."

"Really?" Ned snapped back. "I think your sources are just as jealous as you are."

Speedy took a swing at Ned, missed, and fell to the ground. A couple of guys ran over to help him back up. Weasel put himself between Speed and Ned. "Alright, alright, we'll have a discussion tomorrow morning when everyone has calmed down a little," he said. "I don't know what your friends have been telling you, but our new friend here has done nothing but good for us, and if the big boss likes him, if Poco Loco himself trusts him, we should respect that."

"Yeah, okay, I'll wait 'til tomorrow," Speedy said angrily. "Then you'll hear what El Guason and El Martillo think about this guy." Then he turned to the girls from his bar. "Any of you girls go home with this asshole and you're fired," he yelled. "Got me?"

"I thought I was a fag," Ned quipped, and everyone who heard him laughed, except for Speedy who stormed off.

* * *

The next day, Big Red got up early. It was a habit that his neighbors hated—his pipes woke people for blocks—but none of them had the courage to do anything about it. He revved his big Harley at every stop, delighting in letting everyone know about his presence, not caring what they thought, just being glad they knew he was there. He never wore a helmet—in Arizona, helmets are required only for riders under the age of eighteen—and when a cop noticed him go through a stop sign, he just grinned at him. Big Red felt like he owned the world. His undercover status gave him a get-out-of-jail-free card. His word was all he needed to get out of trouble.

He drove over to where he had heard the Cossacks had a clubhouse. The cinderblock building was painted black. The gun shop up front looked seedy enough, and the rest of the windowless building was dominated by a huge mural of the Cossacks' logo—a cartoon version of a Central Asian warrior, complete with scimitar, shield, and crazed look.

Circling around the building on foot, Big Red examined the remains of the party, which included Scruffy, still sound asleep in his wheelchair. "Hey! Homeless guy!" he shouted, shaking Scruffy's chair. "Wake up, wake up."

"I am awake," he said. "And I'm not homeless, I live in the shop. Who the hell are you?"

"For the next few minutes, you can consider me God," he said, calmly twisting Scruffy's left hand until he could hear the wrist bones getting close to breaking. "Because I have the power of life and death."

Scruffy screamed, and tried to kick his tormentor, but his old legs just wouldn't cooperate. "What do you want?"

"Tell me everything you know about the Cossacks and this will all end."

Scruffy sputtered. "The Cossacks are my friends!"

"Where are your friends now?" Big Red asked, twisting just a touch more. "It's just you and me here now, and I need answers. Who runs the Cossacks?"

"Weasel, Weasel is the top guy here, but he gets his orders from south of the border," Scruffy was screaming in pain, but his weak, ash-coated lungs could produce just muffled cries. "The Jaliscos, the Clown! The Clown!"

Big Red made a mental note to check out Jalisco and clowns on Google when he got back to his own clubhouse. "And why did you have a party last night?" he asked. "Something to celebrate?"

"It was for the new guy, Crash, Colin!"

"Colin? That doesn't sound like a Mexican name."

"It's not, he's not!" Scruffy couldn't scream anymore, it was all he could do to pant out his answers. "A white guy, from back East."

"White guy? What's he doing here?" Cars whizzed by, their drivers and passengers on their way to legitimate work. They either didn't notice what was going on or pretended they didn't.

"Selling coke and meth," Scruffy told him, hating himself for doing it. "Doing great, making huge money."

"Really?" Big Red twisted far enough to break Scruffy's radius bone with a snap. The old man screamed and wept. "Big money? I like the sound of that. Now tell me something that I will love and you will never, ever see me again."

"I heard Weasel talking about a massive deal, on the twenty-first," Scruffy gasped between screams. "The Cossacks have scraped together $18 million to buy enough coke from the Jaliscos to flood Arizona and New Mexico for months."

"Eighteen large? Wow," Big Red asked. "Where's the drop?"

"Crash, he's gonna bring it to the tub in the Coronado. The Mexicans trust him."

"The tub?"

"The bathtub, there's an old bathtub at a spring in the Coronado. It's there to collect drinking water for hikers," Scruffy choked out. "The Cossacks use it to do business with the Mexicans."

Big Red released his grip. "There, that wasn't so bad, now was it?"

Scruffy rubbed his injured hand with his good one and looked at Big Red with utter contempt. "Now leave!" he cried. "You promised!"

"No, I said you'd never see me again." Big Red smiled as he pushed Scruffy into the laneway behind the building then slid a hunting knife through his ribs. Big Red grinned at the thought that his plan was going to make him a lot richer than he had previously hoped.

* * *

Ned was surprised not to see Scruffy as he walked through Stew Bob's shop to the clubhouse. He would have asked Stew Bob, but didn't want to get in a conversation with him. Instead he just nodded hello and entered the Cossacks' lair. Weasel was already in there with Speedy.

"If you're armed, you gotta leave it at the door," Weasel said solemnly.

Ned assured him he wasn't and sat on the couch opposite him, alongside Speedy.

Weasel cleared his throat. "This is a closed meeting to get to the bottom of Speedy's accusations," he said. "You'll both get a chance to speak, and I will have final say. If you have a problem with that, we can take it to Cossacks headquarters in San Diego or down to the boys in Jalisco. Agreed?" Both men nodded. "Speedy, make your claim."

"Well, the first thing is that he's a fag, and we all know that's not allowed," he said. "My guys in Mexico tell me it was a well-known fact and that they called him *tia*—and we all know what that means."

"Crash?"

"I know some of the guys down there thought I was gay because I didn't take advantage of the house girls," he said.

"But I had just been kidnapped and was afraid for my life. Besides, they were young enough to be these guys' daughters and were basically forced to do whatever they said. I'm straight, but I'm not a rapist."

Weasel paused, making it clear he was considering both sides. "Okay, I heard you both," he finally said. "Those guys down there are like animals when it comes to women—they have no respect for them at all. I can't say that I wouldn't indulge a little myself if I was in his place, but I can also understand Crash's point of view. And I saw him at the party with your girls, Speedy, and if he's a queer, he's also a pretty damn good actor. I'm gonna let this one pass unless you have any real evidence."

Speedy blinked back his anger. "Okay, fine. My friends also told me he was a coward and an informant," he said bitterly. "Remember that big shipment that was disrupted? Not only did he cause that, but he ran the second the shooting started."

"Crash?"

"Okay, the first part is just ridiculous—if I was an informant, how come nobody got arrested? The Mexican media might not want to talk about body dumps, but they make damn sure that every fuckin' arrest is on the front page."

"He's got a point," Weasel said. "It wasn't the DEA or the Federales or anything like that, it was Los Zetas or the Sinaloans or some other group who were after the product or the cash. They were not there to make arrests, but to steal and kill our guys. And to accuse Crash of being with another cartel is, I think, kind of stretching things."

"As far as running, where did I run to? I took a truck with more than $6 million in cash back to the ranch house!" Ned was angry now. "And saved a man's life. Poco Loco thanked me himself. That's why I'm even up here."

Weasel quieted him down. "It's true, Speedy," he said. "I spoke to the Clown himself, and he told me that Crash was something special, that he should be taken care of. I gotta trust the Clown, man; certainly more than I would those two drunken *pendejos* you call friends."

Speedy looked angry, but eerily calm. "Okay, fine," he said. "We'll just wait and see. Just remember I warned you."

"Look, Speedy, normally these kinds of accusations lead to expulsion if they are proven unfounded," Weasel said. "But in light of your years of outstanding work . . ."

"Save your breath," Speedy said. "It was him or me, and you chose him, so I'm gone. Just ask yourself, who was he *before* he landed in Mexico."

* * *

Big Red and Nickels were at the door of the Blue Moon Saloon arguing with the club's bouncers when Speedy arrived. "You can't come in here with colors on, man!" Alphonso, the bouncer shouted. "This is a Cossacks joint."

"It's not anymore," Speedy said. "Come on in, boys, your money is good here."

"You heard the man," Big Red said to the bouncers who towered over him. "Now get outta my fuckin' way." The bouncers angrily made room. He followed Speedy. "What did you mean this isn't a Cossacks joint anymore?" he asked.

"The Cossacks can jump off a fuckin' bridge for all I care," he answered.

Big Red smiled. "Then you won't mind a couple of Tortured Souls in here then?"

"Knock yourselves out."

Big Red and Nickels sat at a table near the stage. Two of the dancers approached them immediately. Big Red bought them drinks, but spoke only to Nickels. About an hour passed before Speedy finally approached. Big Red dismissed the girls. "Want to have a word in the back?" Speedy asked.

The two Tortured Souls agreed and followed him into the office. It looked like what you'd expect of a strip joint owned by a small-town biker—cheap furniture with posters of cars and women taped to the walls. Big Red and his lieutenant sat on the couch facing Speedy's desk. "So who are you guys supposed to be anyway?"

"Haven't you heard of us?"

"I guess I haven't."

"Let me fill you in. We're an established but not very large club from Colorado; we like Harleys, fights, women, and beer and not always in that order," Big Red told him. "But there's only so much open road in Colorado if you know what I mean. Mountains get in the way. We thought there would be some opportunities to ride the open road down here in Arizona, especially now that the Hells Angels are a less imposing part of the landscape."

Speedy smiled. "I know what you mean," he said. "With them out of the picture, it's really anyone's game."

"That's not what I heard," said Big Red with a grin. "My sources tell me that this Crash character, some white guy from back east, has the Cossacks way out in front."

Speedy could hardly contain his rage. "That bag of shit?" he said. "He won't last long."

Big Red grinned. "What makes you say that?"

"He's made some powerful enemies."

"Yeah, who besides you?"

"If I'm not wrong, isn't one of them you?"

Chapter Ten

Stew Bob's first job after that morning's meeting was to take out the trash and recycling from the night before, but he put it off for as long as he could. He hated going into the laneway after he had seen rats in there, but it was part of his job and he had to do it. As awful as the rats were, there was something that day that shocked him a lot more. Beside the dumpster was Scuffy's wheelchair, and beside it was Scruffy. His crumpled body lay in front of the wheelchair. Stew Bob—though he instinctively knew Scruffy was already dead—fell to his knees, trying desperately to revive his old friend.

News of Scruffy's murder put the Cossacks on high alert and they returned to the clubhouse for an emergency meeting. Weasel had been particularly affected by the murder of his old friend, who Ned found out was one of the founding members of the club. Scruffy had fallen on hard times since a motorcycle accident lost him the use of his legs, but the Cossacks were dedicated to him and they took care of him.

None of the Cossacks believed Scruffy's death was a botched robbery or other random event. Stew Bob voiced the opinion, shared by several prospects and hangers-on that Speedy could have been involved. The two had never gotten along, and now that Speedy had left the club, he could well have killed Scruffy after leaving the morning meeting, as a twisted sort of revenge.

Weasel wouldn't have it. Despite their differences, he still had a great deal of respect for his old friend Speedy. Besides, he said, he had called Speedy with the news and he had seemed genuinely shocked. And if he had killed Scruffy, why would he stay in town and accept calls from the club's top guy? "It wasn't him," he said with a gravity that suggested an absolute finality to the discussion.

El Borracho mentioned the new club, the Tortured Souls, who had moved into Tucson. "They could be trying to establish themselves here," he said. "A bold move like that would put them on the map."

"Yeah, and it would also be a war," Weasel said. "And from what I've heard and seen, they don't have any manpower or significant friends. It would be suicide on their part."

Ned, who had been one of those who believed Speedy was to blame, mentioned that he had read about the Tortured Souls in the newspaper. "They are pretty small time," he said. "But have more members up in Colorado and some ties to the Outlaws, who are a fairly big club out East, especially in the Chicago-Detroit area and in Florida."

Weasel scoffed at that. "There are no Outlaws around for hundreds, even thousands, of miles," he said. "And, from what I have heard, they're in a worse position than the Hells Angels and Bandidos. If there's a shooting war, they are not going to coming riding over the horizon to save the Tortured Souls like some cavalry troop in an old western movie."

"Could it have been the Mexicans?" Ned asked.

"Which ones?"

"One of the other cartels," he said. "If Jalisco is moving significant amounts of coke and meth through us, it might make sense for one of the others to get at us."

Weasel contemplated that for a moment. "You have a point there," he said. "But Scruffy has been retired for many years. He was of no strategic importance. I don't want to sound disrespectful, but his primary value to the club was sentimental."

"Yeah," piped in El Borracho. "If they really wanted to hurt our business, they would have killed you, Weasel."

* * *

Big Red didn't like the Tortured Souls' clubhouse. It was plenty comfortable inside, but the ATF had filled it full of hidden video cameras and listening devices to make sure everything their agents did was ethical and by the rules. He spent as little time as possible in there and made sure to conduct business that actually mattered outside.

At the same time that the Cossacks were talking about Scruffy's death, Big Red and two of his men took a ride down to Coronado to look for the bathtub. Big Red justified the trip to the other two officers by telling them that he had gathered enough evidence to indicate the bathtub was a primary collection point for over-the-border drug smugglers.

It quickly became apparent that jeans and black T-shirts were a bad choice for hiking in the Southeastern Arizona desert heat. On their half-hour hike, they had run into two different sets of illegal immigrants with bulging backpacks. The officers agreed that they were probably carrying hundreds of thousands of dollars worth of drugs on them, but they didn't arrest them or even report them for fear of jeopardizing their primary purpose. These couriers were small fish—something for Border Patrol or the local Barney Fifes to take care of. Their job, Big Red reminded them, was to bring down the big guys and anything that could compromise their identities would endanger that.

He had not yet revealed to the other officers that it was the Cossacks who were supplying the area with coke and meth. Keeping them busy and out of the loop allowed him time to think and plan out his own strategies. They did not know that the Cossacks' new star drug dealer also just happened to be a rat who was going to help Big Red get rich.

The three officers dressed as bikers were worn out by the time they arrived at the bathtub. Two of them sat, while the fattest, Frank "Lunker" West (originally from Seattle and still bedeviled by the Arizona sun), lay down in the shade. An outdoorsy-looking couple entered the area from a different trail but, upon seeing the Tortured Souls, decided to keep hiking.

"So this is the spot?" West asked. "Sure doesn't look like much."

"It doesn't have to be," Big Red answered. "All these guys need is a familiar landmark—meet me at the bathtub is a pretty clear sentence—it doesn't have to be the Eiffel Tower to be a meeting place."

The other officer, Kellen Rogers (better known by his Tortured Souls nickname, "Dawg"), offered his opinion. "Yeah, when I was working in Cincinnati," he said, "there was an old oak tree everyone knew about—after a while, you could say 'meet me at the tree' and that would be enough."

"So who's moving the stuff through here?" West asked. "Obviously it's one of the cartels moving it up, but who's distributing it on the streets?"

"From what I've been able to uncover, there are a number of gangs on the streets," Rogers said. "Cincos, Los Toltecas, the Cossacks."

"All Mexican," Big Red pointed out. "And they only sell to other Mexicans."

"That's not entirely true," Rogers retorted. "An informant I have told me that the Cossacks are making very significant inroads in the . . ."

"The Cossacks?" Big Red scoffed as convincingly as he could manage. "Don't make me laugh. Those guys couldn't organize a piss-up at a brewery. At best they are mules, ferrying the stuff to the hub up in Denver."

"Well, somebody's putting product on the pavement from Nogales to Tucson and points beyond," piped West. "If it's not the Hells Angels and it's not the Cossacks, then who the hell is it?"

Big Red grinned. "Well, I guess it's our job to find that out, now isn't it?"

* * *

Speedy was in his office going over the payroll when he heard a knock on his door. "What is it?" he shouted. Alphonso, the bouncer who was also his primary assistant, entered. "There's a man here to see you," he told him. "From Mexico, says it's very important."

"You recognize him?"

Alphonso, who had moved to Arizona from Milwaukee only a year earlier felt awkward. To him, many Mexicans actually did look very much alike and he was honestly not entirely sure he had not met this man before. Quickly weighing the odds, Alphonso said that he hadn't.

"Send him in anyway."

Speedy was pleasantly surprised to see Francisco "Frankie X" Beltran Vazquez, his cousin and a brother-in-law of his old friend El Guason. He instructed Alphonso to get some beer and invited Frankie in. "I guess you heard about me and what happened with the Cossacks," Speedy said to him, prepared to apologize. "You'd have done the same thing, though. That Crash *pendejo* just pushed me too far."

Frankie was surprised. "I have no idea what you are talking about."

"I quit the Cossacks," he told him. "I had to. That guy Poco Loco sent up here was screwing everything up, taking everything for himself."

"El Espagueti?" Frankie chuckled. "I'm surprised he's still alive—always seemed like the ultimate fuck-up to me. I can't believe you let him push you around. Trust me, he won't be a problem."

"You don't know, man," Speedy said in his own defense. "He may give the impression he doesn't know what's going on, but he is pretty fucking clever under the surface."

"I do know, my old friend," Frankie smiled. "He's done, you can even kill him yourself if you want to."

"But Poco Loco . . ."

"Is dead."

"What?"

"Yeah, believe it or not, the Clown is dead," Frankie said, grinning widely.

"How?"

"You won't believe this, but El Azucarero, we believe, was in the hands of Los Zetas," Frankie said. "He led the naval infantry and the Federales up to the big house in the mountains near Bambuto. There was a shoot-out and Poco Loco took a couple—well—a couple dozen hits. Some of it was from a .50-caliber, so he was mostly just shreds when they were done with him."

"I can't believe it, I really can't," Speedy said. "But how do you know it was El Azucarero?"

"The fuckin' Zetas put a video up on YouTube bragging about it," he said. "They claimed it was one of Poco Loco's closest confidantes who did him in, and after we counted all the bodies and the men behind bars, the only one missing was El Azucarero."

"His family is going to get a nasty surprise, I'll bet."

"Who cares?"

"What do you mean?" Speedy was shocked. "We must avenge the deaths of Poco Loco and the others."

Frankie laughed. "Sure, whatever," he said. "All I know is that this moves all of us up a couple of notches in the organization at the very least—and we don't have to listen to Poco Loco's annoying neo-communist speeches anymore. I, for one, won't miss him at all."

Speedy acknowledged Frankie's pragmatic point with a chuckle. "I guess you're right. I think that all his politics were keeping us back anyway, nobody who wants to get rich wants to be told what to do by a communist. I sure as hell don't. It was keeping us from getting the best talent," he said. "So who's in charge now?"

"Again, I have to say you are not going to believe this," Frankie said. "It's El Cubano."

"No way!" Speedy's mind reeled. El Cubano was Edgar Beltran Villareal, a first cousin of both Speedy and Frankie X. It was indeed good news. And the look on Speedy's face indicated to Frankie that he understood the sum and the gravity of what had happened.

"Slow down, *Jefe*. We can celebrate later," Frankie said. "But now we have to make a few plans."

"Are you staying up here?"

"Nope, I'm running the ranch house from here on in," he said with pride. "El Ratón got popped. They were gonna give it to El Guason, but he's hitting the bottle pretty heavy, and they need him as a *sicario*—he's still the best we have. No matter how drunk he gets, he just seems to have a talent for killing people."

"And me?"

"I think you know the answer to that," Frankie said. "You should stay up here and move product."

"No, no, no, that's what that *pendejo* Crash is doing," said Speedy. "I quit the Cossacks yesterday."

Frankie chuckled. "You think those customers are loyal to El Espagueti?" he said. "It's drugs we're moving here, and these people have no other choice. We have them, they need them, and now, thanks to your *guero* friend, they know where to get them. They don't need him anymore, they're all grown up now, they can let go."

Speedy laughed. "I'm pretty sure I pissed Weasel off pretty badly, though," he said. "And no matter what anybody says, he is the Cossacks here."

"And he knows how to make money and he definitely knows how to spend money," Frankie said in a reassuring tone. "I'm pretty sure he'll welcome you back to the Cossacks. I think they're going to have a vacant spot soon."

Speedy laughed. Things were looking good for him. Once Crash was out of the picture, he could rejoin the

Cossacks. Or, if the offer was better, he could try the Tortured Souls. Either way, El Cubano would make sure he was well taken care of.

* * *

Weise laughed. Tovar shot him something of a dirty look. "What's so funny?" he asked.

"You," he answered. "You are so excited to see this woman that you're actually speeding."

Tovar laughed. "Shit, you're right—I actually am speeding," he said. "But, I have to admit, I really want to know what she has to say."

The agent and his intern were racing down Highway 19 to interview a woman who had called them that morning. She said she may have recognized the man in their flyer. They made a date to meet her at her home at noon.

It was a nice, well-manicured bungalow in the semi-exclusive Tanque Verde neighborhood in Tuscon's east side. Weise noted the Prius parked outside. They parked in the driveway and approached a woman who was out front, tending her sparse garden.

"Erin Scholtz?" Tovar asked.

"Yes, hello. Are you the man I spoke with on the phone?"

"No, I'm agent Tovar of the FBI, and this is my associate, Mr. Weise," he answered as they both showed their identification. "But we are here about the telephone call."

"The FBI?" she asked, her eyes wide. "Is this man dangerous? Is he a criminal? All I wanted to do was help him. Your advertisement said he was sick, that he needed his medicine."

Weise told Scholtz that she was in no danger and that any information she gave would be totally confidential.

She looked skeptical. "I'm not sure it was even him, this man you're looking for," she said. "Your advertisement said he was sick and needed medicine. The man I saw was the picture of health. He looked very happy, in fact." She went back to tending her garden, forcing them to follow her.

"Where did you see him?" Weise asked.

"Downtown, he was going into one of those fast-food places, Gibby's—or it may have been Sweet Pete's," she said. "They're all the same to me. I would never go into one those places; nothing but sodium, fructose-glucose, and saturated fats on their menus, I'll tell you that. No thanks, Mr. Fast-Food Man, I choose to live healthy."

"It would really help if you could tell us which one."

"I told you I don't know," she snapped. "It was one or the other, but it was on North Campbell around where it hits East Prince."

Tovar knew from experience that there was not only a Gibby's and a Sweet Pete's around that intersection, but several other similar barbeque outlets as well. "Was the man in question riding a motorcycle, like a Harley-Davidson?" he asked. "Did you see anything like that?"

She looked at him like he was crazy. "Oh, this man was definitely not a biker," she said. "Short, tidy hair, no beard, no beer gut, dressed nicely—are you sure we're talking about the same guy?"

"Not everyone who rides a motorcycle looks like that, ma'am," pointed out Weise—himself the proud owner of a Yamaha FZ6R. "Even Harley riders."

She looked at him sternly. "Actually, officer," she said. "I did notice that he came out of a nice car, Volvo I think. Something like that. Not a BMW, but that type. New or very close to it. Black, if it helps."

"It sure does, thank you," said Tovar, smiling. "You didn't happen to get the license plate, did you?"

"No, I was busy and I just looked at him for a second," she said. "I didn't even put together that he was the man in the picture until I came home. I'm sorry I can't be more help."

"No. No, Ms. Scholtz, you've been a great deal of help," Tovar replied.

After they said their good-byes and got back in the car, the two feds started discussing their prospects excitedly. Weise could hardly contain his enthusiasm and his pride in getting the FBI to that part of Arizona in the first place. Tovar was also pretty pumped, but didn't want the kid to get cocky.

"Don't get your hopes up too high, kid, because all we have is a guy who looks like a guy that this woman saw for a second," Tovar said. "But at least we have something on the ground now."

"Yeah, all we have to do is hand out his photo at every fast-food joint on grease alley," Weise said. "If it's him, someone will have seen him and will very likely step forward." Then he paused and asked: "Do you really think it's him?"

Tovar smiled at the intern. "Hard to say. He's not a remarkable-looking guy, and the Volvo? That actually threw me for a loop," he said. "It's not a cheap car by any means, and doesn't exactly scream drug dealer, let alone biker. There was nothing to indicate he had any real money when he left Delaware, so it makes me think it's just another unremarkable-looking guy minding his own business, driving his Volvo, and eating his barbecue."

"But we're still gonna try, right?"

"Of course we will," Tovar assured him. "It's all we have."

* * *

While Frankie was up in Arizona telling Speedy the news about the changes at the top of the Jalisco Cartel, El Cubano (its new leader) was at the ranch house, assessing the organization's strengths and doing his best to boost his men's morale.

The meeting went smoothly. El Guason was acting as regional boss because Speedy was on assignment in Arizona, and he had a great rapport with El Cubano. They spoke about a wide variety of operations, and eventually came to the Cossacks. El Cubano—who had seen the numbers from the operation and was surprised at how quickly it had taken off—was particularly interested in that outfit because it was something the cartel owned and operated essentially on its own, rather than through other larger organizations in the United States. The Cossacks answered directly to them, while the other gangs they used as street-level distributors such as the Lawbreakers, the MS-13, and the Crips never would.

"This thing is becoming big," El Cubano said to El Guason. "We need to repeat this success in other border cities, bigger ones."

"I'd love to do that, too, but most of those cities already have strong networks through organizations like El Barrio Azteca and the White Fence. You even see a few old Mexican mafia members doing their thing."

"And they will have to coexist with the Cossacks," El Cubano answered. "Or get out of the way."

"I like it, but I thought we were keeping as much of our operation on this side of the border as possible," El Guason said, surprised at his new boss's aggressiveness. "We don't want to invite the DEA down here. Look what happened in Colombia."

El Cubano gave him a stern look. "There are many important strategic differences between the two situations," he said. "And it was that kind of head-to-the-ground thinking that kept us working for the Colombians for years. Then suddenly, a few forward-thinking Mexicans took matters into their own hands. That's what I'm doing here."

"But the DEA . . ."

". . . can arrest lots of people in the States, but can't come into Mexico," El Cubano noted with an air of pride. "Here they still have to work with the same Federales and local police who can't stop us now, even with the help of the entire military." He laughed. "What can the Americans do?" he asked "Give them more money, more helicopters and drones? It doesn't matter. We can still pay the people operating them more than they can. They will be ours."

El Guason contemplated the validity and potential of the boss's idea, even though he knew that he was in no place to truly question him. "For this, I think, we will need more *gueros* like El Espagueti," he said in a tone that made it sound like a question. "The thinking among many up there is that he's responsible for their success."

"Really? Is that what he's saying?" El Cubano seemed truly offended. "Typical *guero* attitude, talking all the credit for other people's hard work. Makes me sick."

El Guason just nodded. He had grown somewhat resentful of El Espagueti after the border incident. Like many other people who had actually been there, he interpreted Ned's actions as cowardice and was shocked and angered that he received what was essentially a promotion instead of a punishment from Poco Loco. "So you are telling me that the Cossacks would have succeeded without him?" he asked.

"Totally. Maybe his arrival sparked the others to work harder, but it was largely circumstantial," he said. "People needed some time after the Hells Angels went down to find a new source for product and they eventually found the Cossacks. This will continue to happen if we get more boots on the ground in the U.S. More Cossacks means more money, it's as simple as that. We don't need any *gueros*, just their money."

El Guason had an idea. "What about this particular *guero*, this Espagueti?" he asked."Do we need him?"

"Not at all."

"Then you would not mind if I put that to the test?"

El Cubano chuckled. "Get rid of him, you mean?"

"Yeah, if we don't need him up there," El Guason said. "He's a liability, he knows a whole lot about what goes on down here . . . could be bad for us if the DEA gets their hands on him."

"I'm not afraid of the DEA," El Cubano said. "But I do agree that his continued existence does us no good. Do what you will."

"I'll go up tomorrow."

El Cubano looked shocked. "No you won't. After all the losses we've suffered we absolutely need you here," he said. "Send someone expendable. Someone the organization wouldn't miss."

* * *

Weise knew that canvassing the fast-food joints of Tucson's grease alley wouldn't be fun, but he did not think that he would run into any opposition. While Tovar took the other side of the street, Weise walked into the Gibby's on North Campbell and asked for the manager. "He's not here," said the man behind the counter, who then asked for his order.

The young agent told him he wasn't there to eat, then introduced himself with his FBI identification. He saw the man become visibly disturbed. "Don't worry, this has nothing at all to do with immigration," he assured him. "We just want to put up this poster. We're looking for a man who may be in the area." He showed the man the poster. Again he flinched. Instinctively, Weise took that as an indication that the man knew something. "Can you tell me who's in charge here?"

The man said that he was in charge and that it was against store policy to put wanted posters up. Bad for business, he maintained. Made it look like it was a hangout for criminals.

Weise politely smiled, calmly told the man that he'd be back when the manager was in, and asked when that would be. The man hemmed and hawed then said he didn't know. Weise asked for the manager's name. After a pause, the man behind the counter told him that he did not know the manager's name and that if he wasn't going to order anything he was going to have to ask him to leave.

Shocked, Weise stepped aside and then left the building. An older woman, obese and riding a Rascal mobility scooter followed him out. "Son! Son! Over here!" she shouted. "Lemme see that picture. I spend a lot of time in Gibby's and I see lots of people and lots of things. I see everything."

He handed her the poster. She didn't need to study it for long. "Yeah, that's him, I know that boy," she said. "Comes in about once a week, just hangs out, reads the newspaper, doesn't eat much, just drinks coffee and hangs out. Talks to people occasionally, mostly young people. Lots of women."

"Really? Do you actually know this man? Have you spoken with him?"

"Nah, he's not interested in me," she said laughing. "But he is popular, makes me wonder what business he's in.

How he can afford to sit around doing nothing all day. He must be on disability like me—though I don't see anything wrong with him."

Weise was shocked and delighted. "Excuse me, Ms. . . . Ms. . . . ."

"Heinz, like the ketchup," she piped up brightly. "But there's only one variety of me."

"Excuse me, Ms. Heinz," he said warmly. "What you have here—what you have seen, what you know is very important to us. I'm going to have to call my associate, Agent Tovar, about this right away. Would you have time for a formal interview?"

"I've got nothing but time," she smiled.

* * *

As he rounded the corner to get to Dave's, Ned was surprised to see Hector, the manager, outside. It was incredibly hot outside, and he could see that Hector was sweltering and truly uncomfortable. Ned waved at him and found a parking spot. Hector started to jog over to the Jaguar even before Ned came to a complete stop. Ned lowered the driver's side window.

"Don't come in," Hector told him through the window. "Just keep driving."

"Why? What's going on?"

"Two guys from the FBI—the fuckin' FBI, man—came here looking for you."

"What? No way."

"Yeah, man." Hector's eyes were still very wide. "They left behind a poster with your picture on it, man. It says you are a very sick man and you need your medicine."

"Shit, what name was on it."

"Edward Nelson Aiken," Hector told him. "But it also said you might be known by a bunch of other names; since one of them was 'Crash,' I knew it had to be you."

"Did you say anything? Did anyone?"

Hector scanned the area. "Of course not," he said. "But you gotta get lost right away. I don't want to have to go back to Tamaulipas, man. I got some problems down there."

"Yeah, yeah, I understand." Ned thanked Hector, closed the window and drove north out of the city. He didn't stop until he got to a small coffee shop in Tortolita. In the parking lot behind the restaurant, he dialed Weasel's number.

"I've been waiting for you to call," Weasel said instead of hello.

"So you know, then?"

"Of course I do," Weasel said with obvious frustration. "Yours is the twelfth call about those fuckin' FBI agents already this morning."

"So what do we do?"

"We?" Weasel laughed. "I'm fine, but I think you're about done here . . . gonna have to get scarce pretty soon."

"Pretty soon? I'm leaving now."

"No you aren't," Weasel told him. "You still gotta make the big drop tomorrow."

"What? No way!"

"No, man, this has to happen," Weasel told him. "I just got off the phone with Frankie X—he's a new big man down there—and he knows of the situation and has told me that it absolutely, positively has to be you who makes the drop."

"And if I don't?"

"It's one thing to have the FBI after you. They might put you behind bars," Weasel said, the concern in his voice obvious. "But these guys in Mexico will not rest until they find you then torture you to death if you don't do what they say. Don't be an idiot. Just make the drop and then disappear. I've already talked about it with Frankie; he said everything would be fine."

"I have to think about it."

"No you don't. It's not just $18 million; it's your life now. My life. Everyone's. You absolutely have to do this," Weasel said. "Especially since your friend got popped."

"My friend?"

"Yeah, the Clown," he said. "Federales filled him full of holes yesterday—or didn't your *New York Times* report that?" It had, but Ned hadn't read it yet. He had planned to over lunch in Dave's.

"Poco Loco is dead?" he asked. "Who's in charge now then?"

"Some guy they call 'El Cubano,' I don't know anything about him," he said. "But if he says you gotta go, you gotta go."

"Yeah," Ned said. He hung up and started driving aimlessly before he realized he was deep in the desert, and that if he ran out of gas, he was a goner.

* * *

Unlike most of his cousins south of the border, Speedy had never shot a man. He carried a gun with him most of the time, and had pulled it once at a face-off with some teenage Hells Angels supporters, who slunk away the second they saw the guns.

But he felt like he could kill that day. This Crash guy had brought nothing good with him and he had led to the breakup of the Cossacks, he thought to himself. And, with him out of the way, he and the Cossacks would be free to run things in southeastern Arizona.

Speedy packed an AR-15 and a couple of extra clips in his bag, added a Glock on each hip and put on a Kevlar vest. He knew where Crash lived and, realizing his Harley would draw too much attention, drove his brother's car to the house. After driving around it twice to get a better idea of whether or not anyone was inside, he parked in the alley way behind the yard and jumped the fence. Getting in the back door was no big deal. In fact, Speedy was surprised how little security Crash had on his place.

Once inside, he looked around, determining that he was indeed alone. He shut all the lights off, except the one in the front hallway that had been on when he arrived, and took some night-vision goggles out of the bag with the AR-15. He sat and waited for Ned to come home.

* * *

Stew Bob didn't recognize the man who came into his shop, but was always happy to make new customers. The man, ordinary-looking, wearing jeans, a black Harley-Davidson T-shirt and boots seemed to be checking out the WASR-10s—civilian copies of the AK-47 that were popular in the area. Stew Bob knew that a lot of Americans were being bribed by Mexicans to buy powerful guns for them; in fact, just a week ago one kid bought eight WASR-10s from him, paying almost $3,000 in cash. Stew Bob had a very clear idea as to where the guns were going and what they were being used for, but it wasn't his problem.

He approached the guy. "That's a pretty nice gun you're looking at there," he said. "If you're after an AK-47 copy, I have these guys from Romania, or I can move you up to an Arsenal, assembled in the U.S. from Russian and Bulgarian parts. But if you want to go cheap, you're better off over at Mickey's up the road. I don't carry any of that Chinese shit."

The man shrugged. Then he pulled out a Glock handgun and shot Stew Bob three times in the face.

His body fell forward so quickly that Big Red had to step out of the way to avoid being hit by it.

Weasel had been at his desk back in the clubhouse when he heard the shots. He heard shots in the building all the time—Stew Bob had a firing range in the basement—but these sounded different, as though they came from within the shop. Normally, he wouldn't even have noticed, but all of his senses had been on high alert since Scruffy's body had been discovered. He grabbed his own pistol and went out to investigate.

As quietly as he could, Weasel approached the door to the shop. He grabbed the knob, and as slowly and quietly as possible, he turned it with his left hand. Before applying any pressure to the door, he lifted his right hand, holding his loaded gun, and pointed it at heart level. He opened the door a crack. A shaft of light shot in. "Stew Bob?" he shouted. No answer. "Stew Bob, you in there?" Again nothing.

Weasel opened the door wide. Scanning the room, he saw that the front door was characteristically left open; then he saw Stew Bob's giant corpse facedown in the middle of the shop. Instinctively, he ran to his fallen friend. Big Red, who had been hiding behind the back door, popped out and sent four shells searing through Weasel's back. He was dead before he hit the ground.

Without emotion, Big Red stepped over the dead bodies, shut and locked the door, and turned the "Open" sign on the shop window to "Closed." He then dragged the bodies behind the counter, shut off the lights, and went into the clubhouse to wait.

Chapter Eleven

Ned woke up the next morning in the front seat of the Jaguar. He was parked behind a Taco Bell in some suburb he barely recognized and his fitful sleep had been shattered by the clatter of metal and plastic bins thanks to the guy who carried out the restaurant's garbage. Without thinking, Ned put the key in the ignition and began to drive back to Tucson. He was headed home until he looked to see what time it was. He knew he had to get started on the trip to Coronado soon, so he had better get back to the clubhouse. If it came down to it, he knew he could shower and change there if necessary.

It took him quite a while to get back to the city. A combination of early-morning commuter traffic and his new adherence to speed limits and other traffic laws ensured a slow ride in. The amount of time he took made him even more nervous. But when he finally arrived, he felt a bolt of much-needed confidence when he saw Stew Bob's gigantic Harley and Weasel's truck parked together.

If he had gone around the front, he may have noticed that the store was closed, something that virtually never happened at this time of day. And if he had peeked in the window, he would have seen a pool of blood trailing to a place behind the counter.

But he didn't. Fearing he was late and knowing he had an all-important job to do, Ned went in the back entrance. The lights were off. He shouted for Weasel and Stew Bob, but got no answer. Thinking he may have read his car's clock incorrectly and been early, Ned headed back toward the room with the cot and the shower. He wasn't sure if he'd sleep or shower, but he knew he couldn't just sit around and wait. He was just too stressed.

As he passed through the office, he was stunned by the sight of Big Red sitting behind Weasel's desk and pointing his Glock at Ned's head. "How's it going, Mr. Aiken?"

"Who the . . . Aiken?" Ned shook his head. "Who are you?"

"Just a friend," he said. "Now drop your weapons."

Ned did as he was told, took the gun out of his bag, and placed it on the desk. "That's the only one," he said as calmly as he could manage. "Why did you call me Aiken?"

"Well, the FBI has been putting these posters of your face up all over the place, and since we all like to share information, I thought I'd find out a little bit more about you," he said. "Let's see now, my friends over at the FBI say you were with the Springfield Sons of Satan, ratted them all out, went into rat's protection under the name Eric Steadman then fled after murdering an FBI agent for reasons unknown. That about it? Or is there something you've done here that I should know about?"

"Murder? FBI agent? I never . . ." Ned realized that the man in the chair was probably talking about Dave, his primary FBI contact, whose body he had found back in Delaware. It was actually a professional assassin from the Russian mafia who'd killed the man, but Ned knew he didn't have time to explain what had really happened. He also knew nobody would believe him, so there was no point denying it. "So you're a cop?"

"Something like that."

"And you're arresting me?"

"Well, if I arrest you, I'll get a very pretty ribbon, maybe a raise, and perhaps a promotion some time down the road," he smiled. "I'd much rather have the $18 million."

"I see."

"So where is it?"

"I don't know."

"What do you mean you don't know?"

"I really don't know," he said. "You don't think they'd trust me with that kind of information do you? My instructions were to wait here until my contact told me where it was. Weasel and I are going to take it to Coronado, hook up with some couriers, load the truck, and bring it back here."

Big Red laughed. "Okay, so we wait," he said. "First things first, though. You're going to have to put this on." Then he threw him a small electronic device attached to a flexible strap.

"What's this?"

"We call it a tether; it's an ankle monitor," he told him. "It sends radio signals over cellular phone lines to tell me exactly where you are all the time."

Ned held the device and scoffed. "Don't you need a court order for something like that? Aren't these ankle bracelets all monitored by some kind of central command?"

"Court order? Central command? I'm stealing $18 million, asshole, not putting you in jail—unless you refuse to cooperate," Big Red laughed. "This is just an evaluation device anyway; the only one who will see your comings and goings will be me on my laptop here. Hey, I can see you now." He laughed and pointed at the screen. "Put it on and walk over here so I can make sure it's locked," he said. "And don't worry about Weasel."

Ned did as he was instructed. "So what's your plan?"

"We wait for your phone call, you go get the cash, you bring it to me, and we part company," Big Red said. "Where you go after that doesn't really matter to me. Even though you are an inveterate rat, I know you can't rat on me because if you did you would be facing the gas chamber . . . no, wait, it's lethal injection in Delaware, isn't it? You don't have any friends left with the Mexicans. The bikers are out for your head. You'd be better off just disappearing.

What the hell, maybe I'll give you a few bucks to help that along a little. No, actually, I don't think I will."

The two men sat together in silence on opposite sides of the desk, waiting for Ned's phone to ring. Finally, Big Red broke the tension. "You must be a hell of a lot smarter than you look, getting away with all this for so long," he said. "I mean, I wasn't even looking for you. I just happened to be here in Tucson when I saw your picture in the window of a fast-food place."

Ned sighed. "You're from the Tortured Souls, right?"

"President of the Tortured Souls, my friend."

"Weasel should be back soon," Ned said. "That could be a problem for you."

"Don't worry about Weasel."

"Don't tell me he's in on this, too."

"I'd like to, but he isn't."

Ned's phone rang. When Ned brought it to his ear, Big Red leaned in close so he could hear, digging the barrel of his gun between two of Ned's ribs.

"Yeah," Ned answered.

"Espagueti, it's me, El Martillo."

"Yeah."

"What's the code word?"

"Pozole."

El Martillo's sigh was audible. "Good, good, man, just had to make sure it was you."

"It is."

"You sound strange, Espagueti, is everything okay?"

"Yeah, just nerves."

"Don't worry, man, it gets easier. After a couple of times, you barely even think about it anymore. Just relax. It will all be over soon."

"Yeah, thanks, man. So where do I go?"

"There's a little shop on the south side at 51 South Sunset called Maria's. Go there and ask for Abuelita. She's a tiny old lady, but everyone listens to her because they are totally into the Santa Muerte."

"Santa Muerte?"

"You know, Saint Death, the cult with the skeleton angel?"

"You mean that Grim Reaper thing you see everywhere in Sonora?"

"Don't scoff, man. It's a religion to a lot of people down here and even some up there. Treat it with nothing but the greatest respect around those people or they will leave your dried-up bones in the desert—and only if they want them to be found."

"Understood. Do I have a password when I get there?"

"Nope, just ask for Abuelita."

"Fine."

"Good luck, Espagueti."

"Thanks." Ned hung up.

Big Red went back around his desk. "Okay, I wrote everything down and I've found the address on Google Maps," he said. "If I see you go anywhere other than this Maria's place or if the tether tells me you've tried to take it off, then you are a dead man. I have people—some from the local cops, others from the ATF, and others who just want to be

Tortured Souls—all over the city and the highway who know who you are. On my word, they might just arrest you for the murders of Stewart Robert "Stew Bob" Wisniewski and Edgar "Weasel" Ortiz and bring you back to me, or they might just shoot you on sight. It kind of depends on who it is."

Learning that both Stew Bob and Weasel had been murdered sent a lighting strike of fear through Ned, but the possibility that he might be framed for the killings didn't bother him at all. He was beyond that by this point.

"Why don't you just come along with me?"

"You think I trust those people? Besides, don't you think the president of the Tortured Souls being seen with a member of the Cossacks might raise a few eyebrows?" Big Red laughed. "Now get the hell out of here."

Ned did as he was told. He really didn't like the idea of going to the drop without a gun and contemplated going home to pick one up. He never kept a gun in the car in case he was stopped by cops and searched, and was starting to regret that decision. But he remembered what Big Red had said about deviating from the path, and if he really did have people everywhere, he certainly would have at least one at his house. It was a stupid idea. He would have to go to the pickup on the south side unarmed.

He jumped into the Jaguar and started the engine. Stressed and freaked out, he neglected his customary look into the back seat. In the moment before he shifted the car into drive, he felt an arm around his neck and a gun barrel pressed into the back of his head. "Drive," the man who owned them said.

As soon as they got moving, the man relaxed his grip, but Ned knew the gun was still aimed at him. "Are you a Tortured Soul?" he asked.

"What the hell kind of question is that?" came an answer in heavily accented English.

Ned couldn't help but laugh a bit. What he asked must have sounded absurd. He switched to Spanish. "Who are you?" he asked. "What do you want from me?"

"Never mind. I am here to find El Espagueti, take him to Coronado."

Ned knew he was lying. Weasel was supposed to go with him to Coronado. There no way this guy was going to pop out of the back seat on both of them. That would have been suicide. He knew this guy intended to put a bullet in him as soon as they got away from witnesses. "Whatever they're paying you, I'll double it, triple it, quadruple it," he said. "Whatever you want."

"Can't do it," the man said. "They have my son. Unless I show them pictures of your body, they won't let him go. I'm sorry."

Ned recognized something in his accent. He took a quick scan of the back seat in his rearview mirror. He couldn't make him out well enough to identify in a police lineup, but he could tell the man was Mayan.

And for the first time since this whole adventure began, Ned came up with a real plan. "Do they call you 'El Chango'?"

The man in the back moved so that his eyes met Ned's in the mirror. "Yes, yes they do." Ned could hear emotion in his voice.

"And you hate it, right?"

"What man wants to be called a monkey?"

"You speak Q'eqchi'?"

"No, but you're close. My native tongue is Poqomam—from Guatemala. How do you know about these things?"

"I know because I've been down there and seen how they treat your people. Do you think they'll let you and your son go after this? Don't you think you will always be owned by them? Is that how you want your son to grow up? Ask yourself this: what do they call him?"

"El Changito," the man said.

"And what happens when they let him go, if they actually even let him go?" Ned asked. "They will own you. You know as well as I do that once a criminal gets something from you, they keep taking and taking until there is nothing left to take. And then they put you to work. You will always work for them, and so will your son. Is that what you want?"

"It is a tragedy, but what can I do?"

"If you help me," Ned said. "I can get you all the money you will ever need."

"What good is money without my son?"

"I have an idea that could free your son and give you enough money to escape Mexico," Ned said. "Do you have any serious training as a *sicario*?"

"Better," the man said. "I am a Kaibil, Guatemalan special forces, one of the few clean ones left. When they finally realized I would not take their money, they took my son."

* * *

Believing that he and Weise were close to finding Aiken, Tovar had contacted the local police and state troopers about what the Heinz woman had told them, and they had set up surveillance at every Dave's location in the area. He was surprised to learn that the ATF had already alerted the same organizations about Ned Aiken earlier that day.

At the one Dave's location on North Campbell where Aiken had been positively identified, Tovar began to question the staff about him. None of them claimed to recognize his photo.

After Weise called Philadelphia to tell them what he and Tovar had learned, Meloni had promised to fly out later that day. Tovar welcomed the additional manpower.

* * *

Speedy got tired of waiting at Ned's house. He had long since realized that Ned wasn't coming home, but decided to wait until morning to make his next move. He collected his gear, left by the back door, and went back to his car. He thought he would find Ned at the Cossacks' clubhouse, and even if he didn't, he could discuss with Weasel what the changes in Mexico meant for them all. With Poco Loco, Crash's one and only supporter, out of the picture, it could be the opportunity he was waiting for. And if Weasel didn't like the way things were shaping up, Speedy could go see the Tortured Souls.

* * *

Although he was still far from sure that he would get out of the day alive, Ned had encouraged this latest El Chango to put his gun away and move up to the front seat. They spoke about their mutual hate for the cartels and the tragedy that had befallen Mexico and how it had affected their own countries.

El Chango III told Ned his real name was First Lieutenant Luis Yrigoyen. He had grown up poor in Guatemala and joined the army as soon as he could. He showed great aptitude, spirit, and athleticism as a youth, and eventually found himself in the Kaibiles where he was promoted very quickly. He had even served as part of a UN-sponsored peacekeeping group in the Democratic Republic of Congo. His unit had been ambushed and five of them were killed. He himself had lost a toe. If it had not been for the quick work of a Tunisian combat surgeon, he would have died or at least lost a leg.

By the time he returned to Guatemala, things there had changed. The Mexicans were in charge of the drug trade and they were more aggressive and less tolerant than the Colombians. They had infiltrated every part of Guatemalan society through bribes and violence, including the Kaibiles. Yrigoyen saw many of his fellow officers and men fall victim to assassinations or change sides due to bribery or threats. He vowed to stay true to the cause of a free and independent Guatemala until his only son, eleven-year-old Anibal, was kidnapped.

He received a package at his office containing Anibal's baby finger and the address of an online video. The video showed about a dozen masked men holding guns pointed at Anibal, who was seated on a chair. The spokesman claimed to represent the Rincon-Bravo Organization, and demanded to meet him at a restaurant in Veracruz. There, nine armed men gave him his instructions: all they wanted was a picture of El Espagueti's corpse and Anibal would be set free; otherwise they would continue to send him parts of his son until there were none left. Yrigoyen had no choice.

Yrigoyen's story made it official: with Poco Loco out of the way, the Jaliscos were out to kill him. Since Yrigoyen was either going to do the job he'd been sent to do or be his partner in crime, Ned felt that he had nothing left to fear. So he shared as much of his own story as he remembered. He had been holding so much inside, been lying for so long, he knew he needed someone to tell. Telling the story from the start was an immense relief, although he could see that this man of principle considered him nothing more than a common criminal.

When they arrived at Maria's, Ned was not surprised. It was an old storefront covered in hand-painted signs in Spanish, many of them faded, peeling, or obscured by wrought-iron bars protecting the door and windows. His stomach sank, though, when he saw about a dozen tough-looking guys out front. At least three of them were visibly carrying weapons. They all stared at Ned as he parked the Jaguar, but none of them said anything. He and Yrigoyen got out of the car and walked toward Maria's door.

As they approached, the men surrounded them. The biggest and nastiest-looking one stood directly in front of

Ned, just inches from his face. "May I help you, *Jefe*?" he asked in English.

Ned smiled. "Yes, I'm here to see Abuelita."

All the men laughed. "Stupid Guero and little Chango want to see my grandma. I don't think so." Ned could hear guns cock behind him.

Ned blanched. "I was sent by El Martillo."

Yrigoyen put his hand into his pocket. More guns cocked. The men started yelling warnings in Spanish. Yrigoyen did not stop. Instead of the gun everyone was expecting, he pulled out a small gold figurine. It was Santa Muerte. "We are here to give her this gift."

The big man in front of Ned smiled broadly. "Hey, Chango, you're okay," he shouted.

The guns dropped and the men moved out of the way. Ned and Yrigoyen entered the shop. It was packed full of religious icons and statues, many of them depicting Santa Muerte. They were led to a back room that smelled heavily of incense, weed, and age. In the middle of the room was an elderly woman seated on a pillow and sucking on a bong three feet tall and shaped like Santa Muerte.

Yrigoyen approached and handed her his gift. She looked at it intently. "You must leave, Mayan," she croaked in Spanish. "This is not work for honest men." Two of Abuelita's men escorted Yrigoyen out of the room.

She beckoned for Ned to approach her. "You, there, the white one with no soul," she forced out in English. "Take the bags and the villainy they contain. Take them and never come here again. Leave this place, leave this land."

Ned didn't know what to say. "Thank you?" he offered. He felt hands on his arms, leading him out of the room.

Out in the sunshine, he saw that the men had four black athletic bags. The leader of the group told Ned that he could probably only fit two in the trunk, so the others would have to go in the back seat. Ned said that was fine and double clicked on the Jaguar's key fob to open the trunk lid and doors. The men dutifully loaded the car and went back to where they were before Ned and Yrigoyen arrived.

* * *

Driving past XXX-Caliber, Speedy noticed it was closed. Although he did think it odd, he did not investigate, instead attributing it to Scruffy's death. He knew Stew Bob and Scruffy had been close, and didn't think it would be out of the question for Stew Bob to close up shop that day. As he turned around the corner, he was relieved to see that Weasel's truck was there and Crash's Jaguar wasn't. He took no notice of the presence of Stew Bob's Harley. Before he entered, he called Weasel's cell phone. Tensions were high among the Cossacks and he did not want to set anything off by entering unannounced. There was no answer. But that wasn't too strange. Weasel tended to ignore his phone when he was busy.

He went in the back door, announcing his arrival by shouting: "Weasel, it's just me, man. Speedy," he said. "We have things to talk about." Not hearing an answer, Speedy walked toward the office's open door. "Seriously, man. We need to talk."

As he rounded the corner, three shots hit him in the chest. They were absorbed by his Kevlar vest, but the force of them knocked him violently to the ground. Regaining his senses, he desperately pulled his gun. But it was too late. Quickly aware of why Speedy wasn't dead, Big Red aimed for his head and shot him again three times. One of the bullets severed his carotid artery, sending a cascade of blood in the air and ending his life.

* * *

One of the regulars from the downtown Dave's location came forward and said that she knew the man in the picture, not just from the restaurant, but also from his morning jogs. They had hit it off and had some long conversations about nothing in particular. She said his name wasn't any of those listed on the poster. Instead, he had introduced himself as Colin McCarthy. Tovar pointed out that when someone has that many aliases, one or two more didn't hurt.

The woman—a 21-year-old bank teller named Inez Velasco—said that she first noticed Colin because of his black Jaguar. It was a nice car. She later saw where he lived because she had seen it parked outside.

Tovar froze. If what this woman was saying was true, they had found Aiken's home. He asked her to submit to a formal interview, but first asked if she could take him to the house.

"Sure," she said, "It's up on North Meyer, right by where I live."

* * *

After dragging Speedy's body into the shop and shoving it on top of the others, Big Red ran back to the laptop. When it indicated Ned was driving by, he looked out the window and saw the Jaguar head down the laneway and park. Ned walked out and opened the trunk. He picked up the two black bags full of cash and started to carry them in.

Ned paused when he saw the pool of Speedy's blood on the floor. "Never mind that, some asshole getting up in my business, no loss," Big Red said. "Now, open the bags."

He did as he was told, then shouted *"Ahora!"* Big Red dropped his guard and two shots went into his forehead and out the back of his skull.

Yrigoyen, who had crouched down in the passenger seat when the Jaguar drove by the clubhouse window, snuck out of the car when Ned was entering the building. As soon as Ned had shouted their agreed-upon codeword, the former special-forces soldier jumped into the doorway and made a pair of expert shots.

Big Red was dead. Ned and Yrigoyen had $18 million in cash, but were in a nearly unimaginable amount of trouble.

Chapter Twelve

Ned couldn't help but smile as he watched the waves crash against the miles-long sand beach. He was lost in daydreams when he heard his girlfriend yell at him. "Get to work," she shouted with a smile, her German accent still striking him as humorous. "You have customers waiting."

He worked at Marta's scooter-rental shop not because he needed money, but for an air of legitimacy and to help her out. Money wasn't an object for him at all. All he could carry on his person was about $5 million, and he still had most of it left.

* * *

After Yrigoyen shot and killed Big Red, he and Ned quickly stripped off his shirt. With a black Sharpie, Yrigoyen quickly re-created Ned's tattoos on Big Red's arms and chest. Ned darkened Big Red's hair with shoe polish and, to make him even less recognizable, Yrigoyen shot Big Red in the face again, this time with an AR-15 that was in the office. Even though most of the face was obliterated, they were careful to leave Big Red's blue eyes intact and open as further evidence that the body was actually that of the man the people who paid the Mayan wanted to see dead. Then Yrigoyen and Ned hastily shot a video that showed the body in detail, Ned's Jaguar, and the inside of the Cossacks' clubhouse. As soon as they finished, they posted it to YouTube.

The plan was to have Yrigoyen take half the money with him back to Mexico, show the guys at the ranch house the video, get his son, and escape. The chances of it working were slim.

* * *

The FBI found Aiken's house empty. As they left the building, Tovar's phone rang. It was the local police telling him about the shootings at the Cossacks' clubhouse.

* * *

Over several years, the investigation concluded that Big Red had been murdered in a gunfight with the Cossacks, although he managed to take a few out with him. The only person missing from the picture was Aiken. Since he was known to be a Cossacks associate and to have the means and motive to kill for his freedom, a warrant was issued for his arrest.

Forensic investigators noted hundreds of inconsistencies with evidence, but with all witnesses dead or on the run, there wasn't anyone to make a big fuss. The drawn-on tattoos and hastily darkened hair on Big Red's corpse raised questions, but they were brushed aside over time; he received a posthumous commendation from the ATF. The Cossacks decided to shut down operations in the Tucson area.

The Kuzik investigation went on, but with a new set of junior officers. Frustrated with the FBI, Meloni went to teach criminology at Coastal Carolina University. O'Malley stuck it out, but moved to forensics and away from the field. Due to his connections there and ability to speak Spanish fluently, Tovar was transferred to Phoenix. He accepted under the condition that he could take Weise with him.

* * *

As soon as he could, Yrigoyen set off for the border, which he would try crossing that night. Ned hid in a cheap motel at the Nogales airport for a few days, bribing the owner to keep his mouth shut, and then escaped Arizona through one of the holes in the fence near the Coronado bathtub. He took a bus from Heroica Nogales to Acapulco and hung around the port until he could bribe a freighter's captain into letting him pose as one of the crew. He didn't look much like a Bashir Ibrahimovich, but for the duration of the voyage, that's who he was. He worked hard, but he never, ever took his backpack off or spent a moment without his gun at his side.

When he arrived in Mumbai, he threw his gun in the bay. The immigration officers had no problem with his passport—they still used typewriters and dial telephones, so detecting the expertly done alterations was well beyond them—but they made a huge fuss over the fact that he had not applied for a tourist visa. After hours and hours of debate, he paid a fine of 1,600 rupees with $40 in U.S. currency. The officials were vehement he take his change, even though it amounted to less than a dollar.

From his first impressions, he hated Mumbai. It was hotter than Mexico, crowded, and indescribably filthy, at least where the freighter landed. But it seemed safe somehow, with none of the sinister stares he knew from Mexico. After a few days in Mumbai, he started hanging around with the tourist and expat bar crowd and began to get used to their lifestyle. He even warmed up to the city. But a pair of couples from New Zealand who were traveling together told him that the place to see on India's West Coast was Goa, so he took a train there with them.

He fell in love with the place almost as soon as he stepped off the train. It was full of resorts, nightclubs, and open-air markets on streets that felt safe at any time of the day or night. Ned decided to stay. He met Marta at a fish curry house, hit it off, and eventually moved in with her. Her Belgian ex-husband had gone to prison for insider trading, but she was allowed to keep her business in Goa because she had bought it with her own money, which she had earned as a graphic artist. Her scooter-rental stand was steps away from Vagator Beach and did a decent business. Ned enjoyed working there, dealing with tourists from all over the globe and working on the bikes.

Marta, who had been in India for four years and knew how things worked there, applied for a work visa on Ned's behalf. He was allowed to work for her while it was pending, and with the Indian bureaucracy the way it was, it would take years before any official in New Delhi would even lay eyes on his application let alone do any checking. Part of Ned's job was to do the company's accounting, a fact that made him laugh every time he thought about it, since it was a fear of living out his days as an accountant that had led him to a life of crime.

It was a good life, and Ned felt freer than he ever had before. But he could not put his past entirely behind him. He read the news from Mexico online every day. He also found out that he was wanted in the United States not just for David Kuzik's murder but also for that of someone named Hauser, an undercover ATF agent who the media reported had lost his life after he heroically infiltrated the notorious Tortured Souls biker club. Ned smiled to himself at what a badass serial killer everyone thought he was, even though he had not killed any of those people. He knew intellectually that one day they might track him down, but with the FBI and ATF and all those other acronyms half a world away, he couldn't sweat it. He'd been through too much to worry about what could happen now. Instead of feeling guilty about his past or worrying about his future, he instead chose to enjoy his present.

Some weeks after Ned arrived in India, CNN.com reported that the Jalisco Cartel had been absorbed by the Sinaloa Cartel a few days after El Cubano's severed head was lobbed over the fence of the yard of the prestigious private school his children attended.

Ned searched the Internet almost every day for signs of Yrigoyen. Almost four months after he arrived in Goa, Ned finally came across a video on YouTube called *"El cuento de Chango y El Guero."* In it, a man wearing a plastic Homer Simpson mask sat on what appeared to be a bench in a city square. The place seemed not quite tropical, but warm, like the Carolinas. The architecture was old and classic, predominantly made of white stone. The sound recording on the video was terrible and difficult to make out. The man spoke in Spanish.

"Guero, I want to thank you," he said. "Come here," he said to the camera. The camera moved, as though being set upon a table or something, and a boy appeared from behind it, wearing a Bart Simpson mask. "We left Arizona, left Mexico, and now we are very, very far away. I cannot tell you the name of the country or city we are in, but the people here are nice and not violent at all. Thank you for the money, thank you for my freedom and, most of all, thank you for my son. I hope you are still alive." It ended with both father and son waving at the camera.

Ned noticed the boy was missing the baby finger on his left hand.

Ned looked at the name of the person who posted the video. It was "ElKaibilyHijo." The video had nineteen views and only one comment. It read, in Spanish, "Is it Uruguay?"

Ned smiled.